PUFFIN CANADA

WHISPERS IN HIDING

KATHY KACER is the author of twelve books of historical fiction and non-fiction for young people that deal with the Holocaust. She has won many awards for her writing, including the Silver Birch, the Red Maple, the Hackmatack, and the Jewish Book Award. Kathy lives in Toronto with her husband and two children, and travels around the country speaking about the importance of understanding the Holocaust and keeping its memory alive.

SHARON E. MCKAY has been an author for more than twenty years and in the process has written more than twenty-two fiction and non-fiction books. Her list of award wins and nominations include the Bilson Award, the IODE, the UNESCO International Youth Library, Europe's White Raven Award, and Canada's Governor General's Award.

WHISPERS
in
HIDING

KATHY KACER

AND

SHARON E. McKAY

PUFFIN
CANADA

PUFFIN CANADA

Published by the Penguin Group

Penguin Group (Canada),
90 Eglinton Avenue East, Suite 700, Toronto, Ontario, Canada M4P 2Y3
(a division of Pearson Canada Inc.)

Penguin Group (USA) Inc., 375 Hudson Street, New York, New York 10014, U.S.A.
Penguin Books Ltd, 80 Strand, London WC2R 0RL, England
Penguin Ireland, 25 St Stephen's Green, Dublin 2, Ireland
(a division of Penguin Books Ltd)
Penguin Group (Australia), 250 Camberwell Road, Camberwell,
Victoria 3124, Australia (a division of Pearson Australia Group Pty Ltd)
Penguin Books India Pvt Ltd, 11 Community Centre, Panchsheel Park,
New Delhi – 110 017, India
Penguin Group (NZ), 67 Apollo Drive, Rosedale, North Shore 0745, Auckland,
New Zealand (a division of Pearson New Zealand Ltd)
Penguin Books (South Africa) (Pty) Ltd, 24 Sturdee Avenue, Rosebank,
Johannesburg 2196, South Africa

Penguin Books Ltd, Registered Offices: 80 Strand, London WC2R 0RL, England

Published in Puffin Canada paperback by Penguin Group (Canada),
a division of Pearson Canada Inc., 2010
Published in this edition, 2010

1 2 3 4 5 6 7 8 9 10 (OPM)

Copyright © Sharon E. McKay and Kathy Kacer, 2010

Manufactured in the U.S.A.

ISBN: 978-0-14-317852-1

Library and Archives Canada Cataloguing in Publication data available
upon request to the publisher.

Visit the Penguin Group (Canada) website at www.penguin.ca

Special and corporate bulk purchase rates available; please see
www.penguin.ca/corporatesales or call 1-800-810-3104, ext. 477 or 474

He who saves one life … it is as if he saves an entire universe. He who destroys a life … it is as if he destroys an entire universe.

TALMUD: SANHEDRIN 4:5

CONTENTS

CONTENTS

INTRODUCTION

HIDING WAS NO GAME. "Got you!" meant being sent to a concentration camp or, worse, being killed on the spot, along with those who had tried to keep you safe. To hide meant living in terror every minute of the day for years. To hide meant to go hungry, to be dirty, cold, and completely alone. Such was the life of a Jewish child in hiding in Europe during the Second World War.

As the war progressed, Germany's Nazi Party introduced laws and rules that restricted the freedom of Jewish people. Jews lost their jobs, their homes, their land, and their rights. Jewish children were denied an education and could no longer play safely on city streets. Ghettos were established across Europe to imprison Jews within their own towns and cities. More and more Jewish people were sent to concentration camps, where they would endure forced labour and eventually face death.

When faced with the prospect of deportation to a ghetto or concentration camp, many Jews tried to find ways to hide. But where? And to whom could you, or your parents, turn for help? Who could you trust to keep you safe?

Jewish adults and children tried to conceal their identities. Parents, in an agonizing decision, sometimes handed their children over to orphanages or homes where they might be kept safe. Some left their cities in hopes that smaller towns and villages would be safer. Others sought out Christian friends and neighbours who might offer refuge. There were many obstacles to overcome.

Jewish people needed false documents that would give them new identities or enable them to travel safely from country to country. They often needed to learn a new language to blend in with the local population. Jewish children had to abandon their own religious customs and learn how to behave like Christians, pray like Christians, and *be* Christians. But most of all, Jewish families needed to find Christian rescuers who were willing to risk their own lives to help.

It was a daunting task for Jews to find safe places to hide in the face of rising anti-Semitism and laws making it a crime to help a Jewish family. The Nazi propaganda machine was running at full tilt, proclaiming that Jews carried diseases, and that Jews were responsible for the First World War and even the Black Plague! Today we can see the absurdity of it all, but propaganda and bullying were then, and still are, a deadly combination.

In many countries, there were secret resistance movements. Their mission was to stop Adolf Hitler and his Nazi armies, and to restore power to their own leaders. These organizations did not necessarily set out to help Jews, and in some cases they actively participated in the persecution and killing of Jewish people. However, there were resistance movements that did harbour Jews who were trying to escape, and many Jewish men and women joined as a way to fight back against their Nazi tormentors.

While there were courageous Christians who were selflessly willing to risk their lives for their Jewish friends and neighbours, sadly there were not enough of them. In addition, money was often needed to pay these rescuers, or at least help pay the cost of food and other basic needs, and in the face of unemployment for most Jews, money was precious and hard to come by.

And even if Jewish families were lucky enough to find a safe place to hide, the conditions in these places were often terrible. There was little food, unsanitary surroundings, cramped quarters, and, of course, the constant fear of the knock at the door or a face peering suspiciously through a window.

At the age of thirteen, Charlene Schiff, along with her mother and sister, fled from their ghetto in Poland after hearing rumours that the Nazis were going to destroy it. Charlene survived in the forests, and years later described her experience of hiding and trying to stay alive.

How I lived in the forest … I don't know, but it's an amazing thing, when one is hungry and completely demoralized, you become inventive…. I ate worms. I ate bugs. I ate anything that I could put in my mouth. And I don't know, sometimes I would get very ill. There were some wild mushrooms, I'm sure they were poison…. My stomach was a mess, but I still put it in my mouth because I needed to have something to chew. I drank water from puddles. Snow. Anything that I could get a hold of. Sometimes I would sneak into potato cellars that the farmers have around their villages, and that was a good hiding place because it was a little warmer in the winter. But there were rodents there and all. And … I ate raw rats, yes, I did. Apparently I wanted to live very, very badly, because I did indescribable things. I ate things that no one would dream of being able to. Somehow I survived. I don't know why. I keep asking myself. But I did.[1]

It is difficult to know how many Jewish people survived the war in hiding, but the number is estimated to be in the thousands. Of course, we will never know how many Jews tried to hide and failed—those who were eventually captured or turned over to the Nazi authorities.

---

[1]Selected text from the Charlene Schiff testimony is used with the permission of the United States Holocaust Memorial Museum, Washington, DC.

These are the stories of several Jewish boys and girls who were lucky enough to survive the war in hiding. Theirs are stories of courage and determination, of struggle and resistance. They speak for those who, like them, found a way to live. And they speak for those who did not.

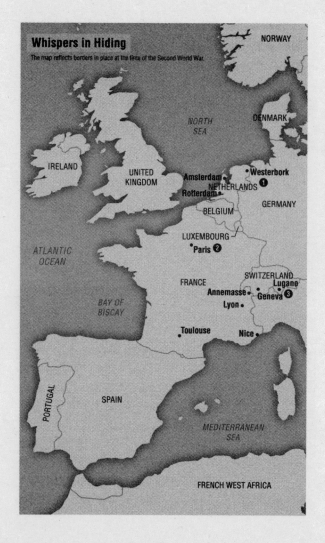

Whispers in Hiding

The map reflects borders in place at the time of the Second World War.

NORWAY

NORTH
SEA

DENMARK

IRELAND

UNITED
KINGDOM

Amsterdam • Westerbork
NETHERLANDS ❶
Rotterdam •

GERMANY

BELGIUM

ATLANTIC
OCEAN

LUXEMBOURG

• Paris ❷

SWITZERLAND
Lugano
FRANCE
Annemasse • • Geneva ❸
Lyon •

BAY OF
BISCAY

• Toulouse   Nice •

PORTUGAL

SPAIN

MEDITERRANEAN
SEA

FRENCH WEST AFRICA

FINLAND

SWEDEN

ESTONIA

LATVIA

LITHUANIA

GERMANY

UNION OF
SOVIET SOCIALIST
REPUBLICS

Rokitno

POLAND

Radom • • **Gorodok**
Lvov •
• **Tluste**

Trawna
• **Humenné**

CZECHOSLOVAKIA

Klačany • • **Budapest**

HUNGARY

ROMANIA

•**San Zenone**

CROATIA

YUGOSLAVIA

BULGARIA

BLACK
SEA

ITALY

ALBANIA

GREECE

AEGEAN
SEA

TURKEY

MALTA (U.K.) MEDITERRANEAN
SEA

BALTIC SEA

ADRIATIC SEA

❶ Netherlands – also referred to as Holland.

❷ The children's home, Château de la Guette, was located close to Paris.

❸ The refugee camp Au Bout du Monde was located close to Geneva.

0   150   300 km

ESCAPE TO RUSSIA

· Poland, 1939 ·

ADAM FUERSTENBERG'S STORY

Left: *Adam as a young boy after the war.*
Right: *Adam's mother and father.*

"TELL ME ABOUT THE TIME we escaped to Russia, Mama," pleaded eight-year-old Adam.

His mother lifted her eyes and gazed lovingly at her young son. "How many times have you heard that story?" she asked as she moved around the room lowering the blinds and folding back the comforter. "Dozens of times? One hundred?"

Adam jumped into bed and pulled his covers up around his chin. "It doesn't matter," he said. "I want to hear it again."

Mama reached over to stroke her young son's cheek. "If I tell you the story, will you go straight to sleep?"

"I promise!" Adam nearly shouted out loud before settling back onto his pillow.

"Fine," Mama replied.

She sounded cross, but Adam knew she wasn't. This was their ritual, the game they regularly played. Adam would beg, and Mama would resist, pretending to be annoyed, before finally giving in to her son and beginning the bedtime story—his favourite. And no matter how many times he heard it, it was still the one he wanted to hear again and again.

"Let's see," Mama said. "How does it begin?"

Adam smiled. He was waiting for that cue. "Tate had already escaped to Lvov, where he got a job in a factory building wooden frames for airplanes," he declared proudly, knowing his father was an excellent carpenter.

"Ah, yes." Mama nodded as she settled onto the bed. "In 1939, your father could see the writing on the wall. He knew it would only be a matter of time before the Nazis came looking for Jews in Poland. He thought he would get across the border to the east and take his chances with the Russians. At the beginning of the German occupation, when the war broke out, everything was in a state of chaos. The border was open, and anybody could cross without written permission. Your father knew this, and he had no difficulty getting through. Your Tate is a wise man."

"And then he wrote you a letter," Adam continued.

"Your father thought all the trouble would end soon, and he would return home. But things only got worse for Jews in Poland. A few months passed and the letter arrived. It said, '*Bring me Adash—*'"

"That's me!" Adam interrupted, and Mama smiled patiently.

"Of course, that's you. The letter said, '*Bring Adash and my parents to me.*'" Mama recited the letter as if it were only yesterday that she had received it.

"I was only ten months old, and I was born on your birthday, March 25," Adam continued.

"You were my birthday present, and we called you Adam because you were the first-born, and a son."

Mama hesitated and closed her eyes while Adam waited, knowing that this was the place in the story where Mama always paused—where she always drifted back in her mind. Adam couldn't possibly remember anything about the time they had escaped. He had only been an infant. But his mother was his memory—his eyes and ears into the past.

A moment later, Mama opened her eyes and continued. "It took a couple of months to get everything together and to make the arrangements. Tate's parents, your Bubie and Zadie, were elderly, and I worried about making this long journey with them. But what choice did I have? I had to go or we would surely have been arrested as well.

3

"By December, my plan was in place and we left our home in Radom. We travelled by train to a village called Gorodok, which was close to the border."

Adam always marvelled at how his mother had begun this journey. By December 1939, train travel had already been restricted for Jews in Poland. German soldiers controlled the railways and were on the lookout for Jews who were trying to escape. But Adam's mother knew how to speak some German, and besides, she could talk herself out of any situation. Maybe the German soldiers felt sorry for her, travelling with a baby and elderly in-laws in tow. Maybe they pitied her. Or maybe they thought, *The fewer Jews in Poland, the better*. And so they turned their backs and let her travel. No one would ever know how it was that Mama managed to get onto the train and out of Radom.

"We arrived in Gorodok, several kilometres away from the border," Mama continued. "I was looking for a farmer whose name was Jerzi Strahofski. I knew that he would help get us across."

"How did you know him, Mama?" asked Adam. "How did you know who to look for?"

Mama shrugged her shoulders. "People in Radom knew of him. I asked questions, snooped around, until I found out about this man. Your mama is a good detective, isn't she?"

Adam smiled. His mother was smart, and he knew it. She had gone to school and learned Latin and Greek. She could

4

recite Polish poetry with ease. But more than that, she was practical, and shrewd. She had what she liked to call *street smarts*.

"But at first, Mr. Strahofski didn't want to help us," Mama said. "'It's too dangerous,' he told me. 'They've become stricter at the border since your husband got across. Besides, the snow is up to your waist. It's too difficult to travel.' He looked at Bubie and Zadie. 'They're old,' he added. 'How will they ever make the difficult trip? And your baby is too young.' Mr. Strahofski shook his head. 'No,' he said, 'if we try to get across the border, the Russians will shoot you, and then they'll shoot me. If you want to go on your own, then go. But I won't be a part of it. I won't help you.'"

"So, you begged him, didn't you, Mama?"

"I begged, I pleaded, I cried. And nothing worked. I told Mr. Strahofski I would pay him a lot of money to take us across. And do you know what he said? He said, 'Money isn't worth anything to me.' And he was right. Money wasn't going to save his skin if the soldiers decided to shoot him. I had run out of arguments. I thought we were doomed and we would never get to your father."

"And then he looked at your boots," Adam proclaimed triumphantly.

"Adashu, do you want to tell this story, or shall I?"

Adam smiled and settled back in his bed, while Mama continued talking.

"I was just about to turn away from Mr. Strahofski. I was going to get back on the train and return to Radom when, miraculously, he happened to glance down at my feet. Yes, that's when he noticed my brown leather boots. In fact, most people in Radom had nice shoes and nice boots. Radom had many factories that cured leather and manufactured shoes. Mr. Strahofski didn't know this. He took one look at my warm leather boots and he said, 'Money is worthless, but your boots—they might be useful to me.'

"At first, I couldn't believe what I was hearing. My boots! I nearly laughed in the farmer's face. But then I realized what he was saying. The boots were of great value. He could have traded my boots for a cow in those days! I realized I had something to bargain with again. Besides, little did he know, I had another pair of boots in my suitcase. I would not miss these. And so, I said to Mr. Strahofski, 'I'll give you the boots on one condition. You take me and my family across the border.'

"Well, Mr. Strahofski paused and thought about this for a long time. Finally, he faced me and said, 'I'll take you one kilometre from the border. That's as close as I'm willing to go. From there, you're on your own. Take it or leave it.' Something told me this was the best I was going to be able to do. And so I nodded, shook hands with Mr. Strahofski, and said, 'Agreed!'"

Adam let out a slow breath. This was the part of the story where his heart always raced and his mind exploded with questions. What would have happened if the farmer had refused to take them to the border? What would have happened if they had been forced to return to Radom? Would he and his family have been arrested, maybe even killed? Adam knew, from other stories his parents had told, that millions of Jews in Poland had been killed in the concentration camps that the Nazis set up. Perhaps he and his family would have been among those numbers. He would not be here, then, listening to his mother tell this story. What would have happened if Adam's mother had not been so smart, or so persuasive?

"We stayed with Mr. Strahofski that night, and early the next morning we left for the border," Mama continued. "It was snowing hard, and we had to sit on the back of the farmer's hay wagon. It wasn't covered and we were completely exposed. The wind was blowing the snow so hard I could barely see Bubie and Zadie sitting across from me. I don't know how Mr. Strahofski was able to see where we were going. On either side of the road, the snow rose in little mountains so high I had to strain to see over them. The rough country road beneath us rocked the wagon from side to side. I was afraid you might bounce out of my arms. So I held you tightly with one arm, and with the other I clutched the side of the wagon and tried to keep from being thrown. It was a terrible journey."

"But that wasn't the worst part, was it, Mama?" asked Adam.

"No, Adashu. It certainly was not." Mama shook her head and took a deep breath before continuing. "We travelled like that for several hours. I didn't know where we were. I had put all my trust in a strange man who promised he would keep us safe. But I had no idea where he was leading us.

"At about noon, the wagon finally slowed and came to a stop. Mr. Strahofski turned and ordered us to get off. 'Keep walking in that direction and you'll get to the border,' he said, pointing farther down the road. I gave him my boots, and with that, he turned the wagon around and disappeared, leaving us alone on the road. We picked up our cases and started to walk. The farmer had said it was only one kilometre to the border, but I have to tell you, it was the longest and hardest kilometre I have ever walked."

This part of the story always made Adam smile, in spite of himself. His mother was strong-minded—that part was true. But she was not in good physical shape. In his whole life, Adam had never seen his mother run. And even when she walked, Adam could only describe it as a waddle. He imagined what she must have looked like, shuffling along the snowy road, carrying an infant and a big suitcase. As desperate as her situation was, the image Adam had of her in his mind was comical.

"I'll admit to you now that I was scared, Adashu. Here I was, a young woman with a baby and two old people. You were crying in my arms, and even though I had some milk

8

from the farmer, there was little else for us to eat. I was already exhausted from coming this far, and I didn't really know how long we would be hiking. The snow was packed down on the road from wagons that had travelled that way earlier, but it was still hard to walk on it. I can tell you now that I wanted to give up, to sit down by the side of the road and just stay there. But the one thing that got me through— the one thing that kept me going—was imagining your Tate's face and seeing the letter that he had sent me. '*Bring me Adash*,' it said. Your father was waiting for us, and I could not let him down.

"It felt as if we hiked for hours, and finally, just as it was beginning to grow dark, I saw ahead of us a wooden rail across the road and a small guardhouse behind it. We had made it to the border. Two Russian soldiers stood guard behind the rail. I was so excited to see them that I didn't even notice that they had their guns pointed at us!

"'Turn around and go back to where you came from. We'll shoot you if you take one more step,' they shouted as we approached. I wasn't prepared for their greeting. I thought they would open the gate and happily let us in. Their words stopped me in my tracks. But instead of turning around, I shouted back at them. 'Go ahead,' I said. '*Strillay!* Shoot me!'"

"You weren't going to go back, were you, Mama?"

"At that point, nothing was going to stop me. I knew I had to convince these soldiers to let us in. Lucky for me, I spoke some Russian. So I said, 'I must get to my husband. He's working in Russia building planes.'

"The soldiers didn't care about this. One of them shouted, 'Who are you?' and I replied, 'I'm just a woman with a baby and my old parents.'

"'Don't come any further,' he ordered.

"'But we're Jews,' I said. 'We need help.'

"They still wouldn't budge. 'It doesn't matter who you are,' the soldier said. 'No more Polish refugees!'

"What could I do? I wasn't going to turn around and start walking away. We would die in the snow before we reached the town we had left behind. So I took a deep breath, stood up as tall and straight as I could, and said, 'I'm coming closer. I'm not going back.'

"Perhaps the soldiers were impressed that your mama spoke such good Russian. Or maybe they felt sorry for me. I must have looked quite the sight, struggling with the case and with you in my arms. Or maybe it was just because, once again, I refused to back down. There was nothing else for them to do except shoot me, because I was certainly not going to walk away. We faced one another, the soldiers and I, and finally, they lifted the wooden rail and told us to follow them."

"It wasn't over yet, was it, Mama?" Adam knew that the most amazing part of the story was still to come.

Mama smiled. "The soldiers led us to their headquarters on a nearby estate. There were trucks, horses, and wagons everywhere on the property, and Russian soldiers patrolling in front of the large farmhouse. That first blast of warm air when we entered the house was such a relief. I felt strong once more and ready to face the next challenge.

"We followed the soldiers into a large room and there, seated behind a desk, was a Russian officer—a colonel. When we first entered the room, he didn't budge. He continued to sit, reading a document and writing something in a notebook. Other soldiers and officers stood around the room. Finally, the colonel looked up, then slowly stood and walked out from behind the desk to face us. The first words out of his mouth were harsh and ugly. He cursed us in Russian and declared that we would not be able to stay. He didn't care who your Tate was, or what he was doing in his country. As far as he was concerned, we were just like all the other Polish refugees who were trying to escape. 'We don't need people like you in Russia,' he shouted. There was no way he was going to let us in.

"I tried everything, Adashu—every argument in the book—but nothing would budge this man. He continued to shout and wave his arms until I felt my last ounce of strength disappear. And then, I stood with my head down in front of this colonel waiting to hear what was going to happen to us.

"Finally, he turned to one of the sergeants in the room and said, 'Get rid of this garbage. We don't want them here.'

"I thought it was the end for us. I thought we were going to be taken somewhere and shot. I couldn't look at Bubie and Zadie. I couldn't bear to think about what was going to happen to you, my darling boy. I couldn't think about your Tate, and how he was waiting for us. We followed the sergeant out of the room and back outside. No words came out of my mouth. I had no arguments left. I felt hopeless and desperate, but there was nothing I could do."

"And that's when the sergeant stopped and spoke to you," Adam said.

"Yes," Mama replied. "That was the most remarkable moment of all. As soon as we walked outside, as soon as we were out of earshot of anyone else, this sergeant turned to me and whispered in my ear. And do you know what he told me? He said, '*On Yvray*. He's a Jew.' At first, I didn't know what he was talking about. 'Who?' I asked. And the sergeant replied, 'The colonel. He's a Jew. *Ya tozhe*. And so am I.'

"All that cursing, all the yelling, had been for effect, so that no one would know that the colonel was Jewish and was prepared to help us. He was one of us, and so was this sergeant whom he had assigned to take us outside. I was speechless. I must have looked quite the sight, with my mouth open, saying nothing.

"'Don't worry,' the sergeant continued. 'I'm going to take you to a farmer who lives close by. You'll be safe there, and the farmer will help you get to Lvov and to your husband.'"

"And that's what he did, right?" Adam asked.

"Yes, that's exactly what he did. He took us to meet the farmer who went with us to Lvov. And there, we were reunited with your Tate." Mama finished the story with a triumphant wave of her hand.

"And tell me again what Tate said as soon as he saw me," Adam begged. It was the last part of the story, and the most important piece of all.

Mama said, "He took you in his arms, he looked at me, and he said, 'Thank you for bringing me my Adash.'"

"And that's why I'm here today." Adam lay back on his pillow with a contented smile.

"That's why we're all here," said Mama.

POSTSCRIPT

It is estimated that more than 300,000 Jews escaped into the Soviet Union after the German invasion of Poland in September 1939. At first, the Soviets left the border open and people could cross freely. But after October 1939, the border was completely sealed and it became increasingly difficult for Jews to cross.

Once inside Russia, these Jews still had great difficulty surviving. Many were sent into slave labour and died. Many joined the Russian Red Army, or Partisan units, and were killed in battle.

In December 1939, Adam's family was reunited in Lvov. In May 1940, they were taken to a Russian labour camp in Siberia. They stayed there for twenty-one months, and in the spring of 1942 they were released.

Adam's family had relatives in middle Asia. They went to Kazakhstan and then Uzbekistan, where they stayed until the end of the war. During that time, Adam's father was drafted into the Soviet army.

In December 1951, Adam and his parents, Regina and Henry, came to Canada. They spent ten years in Montreal, where Adam received a bachelor's degree in English and history from Sir George Williams University in Montreal, which later became Concordia University. After receiving his master's degree in English from the University of Buffalo, Adam moved to Toronto. He taught for many years and is now professor emeritus at Ryerson University. He is known as an authority on Canadian literature and Yiddish literature. For a number of years, Adam was the director of the Holocaust Centre of Toronto. He is married and has three children and one grandchild.

ITALY'S ROYALTY: THE PEASANTS OF SAN ZENONE

· Italy, 1943 ·

ESTHER SCHWABENITZ BEM'S STORY

Esther in Zagreb, Croatia (former Yugoslavia), 1947.

THE PADRE STOOD with his back to the door. His black cassock swept the floor and his white collar circled his throat so tightly that thirteen-year-old Esther thought he must have trouble swallowing. He was a good-looking man, so tall and regal, a hero, *her* hero. He had saved Tata, Mama, and herself time and time again by finding new hiding places for them. He was—Esther could hardly mouth the word—*wonderful*.

"*Tu e anche i tuoi genitori devono avere Tessere, non solo carte da identita. E molto, molto importante.*" The Padre spoke in Italian directly to Esther.

"Esther, what did the Padre just say?"

Esther, Tata, and Mama all spoke both Croatian and German. But Esther's Mama and Tata spoke only a very little Italian, hardly any words at all. Luckily, Esther spoke Italian like a native, and so the Padre spoke in Italian to Esther, and Esther translated his words into Croatian. It was all rather funny, how they communicated with each other.

"Tata, the Padre said that people in the village are beginning to talk about us. He said that our false identity cards are not enough. We need ration cards."

Did the villagers suspect that they were Jewish? That they were on the run? Of course, Esther and her family knew the danger of being discovered. Even here, where Italians welcomed strangers, it was possible that someone might turn them in. It was 1943, and anything was possible now.

"It seems strange to the villagers that a girl your age does not go to school, Esther, and that your mother is not seen in the general store," said the Padre. "You must go to the city hall and apply for ration cards. It must be you."

Ration cards would mean they could get their own food and not have to depend on handouts from the people who hid them.

What if I make a mistake? She could not say the words but they hung in the air nevertheless. *What if I fail?* Esther looked to her Tata, then to Mama, and finally back to the pearly grey eyes of the Padre.

The Padre shook his head. "You must speak for your parents. You must say that the train you were on was bombed. Everything—your clothes and bags and ration cards—was left on the train. And tell them that your father is mute because of the shock of the bombing, and that your mother has lost her voice." The Padre's eyes turned dark as slate.

It was unlike the Padre to speak so plainly, so forcefully, but then so much was at stake. They were hiding in the home of two old people who were illiterate, but devout Catholics. The old woman had more toes than teeth, and the old man was as blind as a stone. Yet, when the Padre had told them that Tata, Mama, and Esther were relatives of his, they had welcomed Esther's family into their home. They trusted their priest with their whole hearts. If the Germans found out that there was a Jewish family living among them, though, then everyone—the Padre, the old people, maybe the whole village—would be shot or hanged in the village square. It had happened before in other towns and other places.

"Come, Esther. You have to try." The Padre spoke quietly and gently.

Esther looked up at him. Like the old couple, she trusted him totally. He visited her family often and brought food—a few eggs, perhaps—and books, oh, glorious books! So what if the books were about Catholic saints? At least they were stories. He understood how lonely she was, what it was like to be in hiding, to be scared all the time, to be hungry. He told them happy stories and gave them hope.

"Esther, I am waiting for an answer." The Padre bent his long frame down and cupped Esther's chin in his hand. "You must, *Elsa*." Elsa was her Italian name, not Esther. Elsa, Elena, and Arturo Tomino were their new names. They had not only left their home, their books, their furniture, their *lives* in Croatia … they had left their names as well.

"Yes, yes, I can do it." Esther smiled at the Padre. He believed in her, and she believed in herself too, most of the time. But yes, she was sure she could do it … almost sure.

"Tomorrow, then." And with a sad smile the Padre left.

Esther climbed the ladder up to the attic. Tata and Mama slept in one bed and Esther in a little narrow cot pushed to the side. It had been two years since they had left their home, and they had now spent eight months in hiding. It seemed like forever!

In Croatia they had lived in a nice apartment and had lots to eat. They'd gone to movies and parties, and Esther had gone to school and had pretty clothes and her own bedroom. Mama and Tata had been happy then. She was sure of it. But it was all such a long time ago.

The Germans, in steel helmets and black boots, had invaded Croatia in September 1941. With them came new laws, more every day. Jews were not permitted to hold any government offices. Jews must leave their jobs. Jews must not frequent public parks. Jews must not ... not ... *not!* People were disappearing. Young men with lives ahead of them were carted off to work for the German military machine and never heard from again. Gone. Vanished.

Every day, life in Croatia had become more and more difficult. Finally, Tata had agreed that they needed to escape. But how? Tata was an engineer, but he wasn't allowed to work. He met a German officer. The German officer agreed to help them, but for a price. Tata had to give him all the gold they had, precious family heirlooms from Esther's grandparents and even great-grandparents. The German officer wanted everything, even Tata's wedding ring. He was an awful man, but he kept his word and helped them get to Italy. And here they had stayed for two long years.

At first, the Italian government had tolerated Jews, as long as they stayed put and did not take jobs away from the local people. But in 1943, the Germans occupied northern Italy, and it was clear that they would not be so accepting. With danger close at hand, the Underground supplied Esther and her parents with false papers. They told Tata that there was a man, a priest, who would help them. They must run again, but where?

Then one night a knock had come at the door. Poor Mama nearly froze with fright. A Fascist, a man who supported the Italian dictator Mussolini, stood in the doorway. He said that he had attended a meeting that very night and had come to warn them. The Nazis had issued an order. "Tomorrow, all Jews will be rounded up and sent to Rome, and from Rome they will go …" He didn't need to finish that sentence. Everyone knew. From Rome they would be sent to camps. Esther didn't know a lot about those camps except that people who went there didn't come back.

They fled. Esther and her parents walked through forests and climbed hills. Their feet and hands were blistered. They were cold, hungry, and tired, so tired. But it was hard to feel physical pain, Esther thought, when she was so very, very scared. For eight months they lived like fugitives, hiding in barns, in caves in the mountains, and sometimes in the homes of farmers too. Finally they arrived on the outskirts of a pretty little village called San Zenone, and there they met the priest—the Padre, they called him. They were lucky beyond belief. It was all about luck. By now Esther—no, Elsa, *always say Elsa*—knew about luck, and that one day their luck would run out.

Esther lay in her narrow little cot. If only there were a window. If only she could see the moon. If only she could be a child again, a real child who went to school and had parents who didn't depend on her. If only the Nazis did not exist. If only she didn't have to go to the city hall tomorrow. She must not think about what could go wrong. She had to chase away her doubts. It would not be so bad. All she had to do was meet with a city clerk, answer his questions, and then he would give them papers.

But something *was* wrong. Esther's stomach twisted. Something bad was about to happen, something very bad.

Elsa—*my name is Elsa, not Esther*—patted down her hair, smoothed her dress, and slipped her feet into her clogs. She could do this, she could. After all this time hiding with nothing to do, this at least was exciting. That was how she would think of it … as an adventure.

"Come, it is time." Tata stood on the threshold. Esther heard her mother quietly utter a blessing as she and Tata set out towards the centre of the village.

The town hall was a large building with broad, thick stone steps that led up to huge wooden doors. Tata and Esther did not speak, not even in whispers, as they climbed the steps.

The doors swung open and Esther all but cried out. Why had they not told her? Why had they not warned her? *No, no!* she wanted to scream. *I can't go in there!* Flags, huge Nazi swastikas, red and white with that evil black symbol in the middle, hung down from the vaulted ceiling. Pictures of the

Führer, Hitler, such a small, ugly man, were plastered over wall after wall.

"Elsa," Tata whispered. He remembered to use her Italian name. He placed his hand, ever so gently, on her shoulder. *Move feet, move.* Esther willed herself forward but inside she wanted to turn and run and run and run forever.

"*Signorina?*" A small man sitting behind a small desk looked up at Esther quizzically. He asked for her papers.

"*Abbiamo documenti.*" Esther held out their false identity papers. They fluttered in her hand. No matter how hard she tried, she could not stop shaking.

The man examined them, muttered to himself, and pursed his lips before handing them back. Then he asked the purpose of her visit to San Zenone. Esther opened her mouth and the story the Padre had taught her spilled out in one long, rambling sentence. Their train was bombed … her father could not speak, it was the trauma … lost ration cards …

The man held up a flat palm and said, "*Si, si.* Wait here." His shoes squeaked on the marble floor as he made his way towards two tall doors. The doors rattled on their hinges as they opened and closed behind him. Then nothing. The silence was so loud that Esther wanted to cup her hands over her ears. She looked at Tata—not square in the face, not in the eyes, but she could see him well enough. She could see that he was as pale as a ghost.

The little man returned, but this time he flung open the two doors and stood to one side. "Enter."

Again, the voice in Elsa's head screamed at her to run, but she stepped forward into a huge and magnificent room. A blond, good-looking German officer, with his feet propped up on an ornately carved desk, motioned her forward with a wave of his hand. She passed more flags and more photographs of Hitler.

Step, step, closer, closer. No, no it couldn't be! He was SS—part of Hitler's elite, the worst of the worst! There was another man in the room too. He wore a black suit and stood directly behind the officer. He was older, about Tata's age.

The officer, taking his feet off the desk, clasped his hands and leaned forward. "*Wer bist du und was willst du?*"

German, he was speaking German. He wanted to know who they were and what they wanted. Think. Think. Her heart pounded in her ears. She was Elsa Tomino, an Italian Catholic girl. Italian girls did not speak German. Think. Tata, she wanted Tata to tell her what to do. Tata spoke German; he, too, would know what the officer had said. She couldn't look at her father. If she did she would crack into a million pieces. *Say nothing, say nothing.* If only she could breathe.

"*Wer bist du und was willst du?*" The officer spoke again but louder now. He was annoyed.

Slowly, with a confused look on her face, Elsa, not Esther,

said in perfect Italian, "*Non comprendo,*" telling him that she did not understand.

The man in the black suit was Italian, a translator. And so the interview continued. The German officer asked questions in German. Where was the train bombed? What did they do after the incident? Where did they go?

Elsa listened carefully. Between the German words and the Italian translation she had time to think about her answers, think carefully. She had been in a train station before and knew that there were always restaurants for travellers. "After the accident we went into the restaurant in the train station. It was then that we discovered that our ration cards were lost." Was she really speaking? How could she sound so confident on the outside when she was trembling and shivering on the inside?

More questions, more answers. Then silence as the SS officer stared at the two of them. His eyes drifted up and down, up and down, then stopped as he looked them square in the face.

Esther took a breath. Did he know they were Jewish? What would he do if he did know? He would kill them, and the priest too, and the old people, she was sure of it. Her mind was racing. But wouldn't the people of the town get mad if he killed their priest? Would they riot? There were hardly any other Nazi soldiers in the town. How many German soldiers would it take to kill a whole town? This man was a killer—all SS men were monsters. But what if he *liked* living in this town? What if he didn't want to upset things? Her heart thumped in her ears. If only he would speak.

Standing on the steps of the city hall, Esther gazed out into the village of San Zenone and felt the sun on her face. Not far away was Venice, the city of lights and music, and in Tata's hand were their ration cards.

POSTSCRIPT

After two years in hiding in the village of San Zenone, the Jewish Brigade liberated Esther and her parents in May 1945. Forever after Esther would refer to the Italians who saved her and her parents as "royalty." In Esther's words, "The peasants of our beautiful village were fearless in the face of oppression."

The Red Cross told them that Esther's sister, Vera, was alive. Vera had fought in Yugoslavia in the Partisan Army of Marshal Tito, had become an officer, and was decorated for bravery. Jelka, Esther's other sister, joined the Partisans in Bosnia and, sadly, had been captured in 1942 and executed.

After a hiatus of four years, Esther returned to school. The transition to freedom, her real identity, and the return to Judaism was difficult.

Esther met Mirko right after the war and married him in Israel. Mirko was a survivor of Bergen-Belsen and Theresienstadt. They have two children and eight grandchildren.

Mirko died at the age of forty-nine. Esther also has two stepchildren and six step-grandchildren.

JEWS OF THE FOREST

• Poland, 1943 •

ALEXANDER (JOSHUA) LEVIN'S STORY

Alex in Rokitno, Poland, with a liberator, January 1944.

"*I'll tell you now, the forest was my family, my home, and my temple. It sheltered me, it protected me, and it fed me as best it could. When I think of God, I think of the forest. I thought I should tell you this before I share my story.*"

—*ALEXANDER (JOSHUA) LEVIN*

THE FOREST WAS ALWAYS OUT THERE, impenetrable, often inaccessible, and always mysterious. In the forest there were caves, lakes, pastures, hills, and bluffs, and trails that ran almost forever. The forest circled Alex's town of Rokitno like a scarf. And just beyond the stately trees, the majestic seventy-five-year-old pines and one-hundred-year-old oaks, was Mother Russia.

Rokitno, in Poland, was such a small place that it was almost hidden from the world. There were maybe 8,500 people in the town, and only 1,800 of them were Jews. It was humble but it was home, and the people had everything they needed. There was a Catholic school and a Jewish school too. There were churches and a synagogue, and everyone said good morning to each other. Children rolled hoops on the road, played tag, and when it rained they floated paper boats in the gutters. Christian and Jewish children played together. Rokitno wasn't pretty—railway towns seldom are—but it was a peaceful place to grow up. For the Levin boys—Natan, Alex, Sam, and Moshe—and for their parents, life was good.

School, on the other hand, was not so good, at least not for seven-year-old Alex. Weekdays were spent sitting on the floor at *cheder*, his Jewish school, and getting whacked with a stick by the rabbi. Alex hated school with a passion.

"You have to listen," said Sam, older brother by a year and therefore much wiser.

Listen? thought Alex. The rabbi was boring. Why listen to a dull old rabbi when they could be outside playing!

Sam came up with an idea. "We'll put on a show. I'll play my violin and we'll charge admission. Everyone must pay a button, and if they don't have a button, well ..." he pondered, "then they get in free."

Lots of children showed up for the show. They tromped around the back garden, past the chicken coop, and plunked themselves in front of the cows in the barn to cheer Sam on. They cheered louder when Sam made the violin squeak like a mouse.

But change was coming to the easygoing way of life in Rokitno. In Germany, Hitler and his evil cohorts were dividing up countries, trading people's land, homes, and lives as if they were a handful of odd buttons. In September 1939, Alex's little part of Poland was handed over to Russia. One day they were Polish, the next day they were Russian!

The Russians, riding on gigantic horses and perched aloft thundering trucks, tossed candy to the crowds that gathered to witness their arrival. The soldiers looked brave and grand in their uniforms, wearing their tall caps with blazing red stars. Such a spectacle! But the best was yet to come. The Russians closed the schools, and the churches and the synagogues too. Hooray! No more rabbi with his stick. Alex could play all day.

Of course, it didn't last. Soon, much to Alex's disappointment, all children, Catholic and Jews alike, were forced to go to Ukrainian or Russian schools.

Again, things changed. The Russians and Germans stopped getting along. In June 1941, the Nazis flew over in their airplanes and bombed the railway station. There were cries from every corner of the village. What to do now?

"We must retreat along with the Russians. We must leave with them now!" Natan, nineteen and the oldest brother in the family, pleaded with Papa.

But Papa disagreed. Hadn't they survived occupation before? The Russians were not so bad; the Germans would likely be much the same.

"Best to stay put," said Papa, and Mama agreed. Natan argued with him through the night, but Papa was adamant. "We are a small town. What do the Nazis care about us? The Third Reich is a powerful empire. Surely they have better things to do than bother a few poor families on the edge of their kingdom."

"But the Nazis do not like Jews. Please, Papa, we have to leave," Natan begged.

"So they don't like Jews. What can they do? And remember, gossip passed from mouth to mouth should not be trusted," said Papa. "I was born here. Your grandparents were born here. Why should I leave my home? Besides, what would we do in Russia? How would we eat? Where would we live? Are we to become beggars on the road when we have a good home and a good life right here? We Jews have survived worse than the Nazis." Such was Papa's reasoning.

There was nothing more Natan could do to convince him. Natan left on his own and was long gone when the Nazis arrived.

The Germans marched in waving swastika flags and wearing hobnailed boots and menacing expressions. Before anyone could catch their breath, a pogrom had been organized, an attack on Jewish homes. Houses were looted and people were beaten and terrorized. People who had once been neighbours and friends wanted the money they said the Jews were hoarding. What hoarding? The Jews of Rokitno were no more rich or poor than their Polish or Ukrainian neighbours. And yet, what few valuable possessions the Jewish families had were carted off on the backs of the looters and Nazi collaborators.

A ghetto was organized just one month after the Nazis took charge. All the Jews would now live on two streets. But how could 1,800 people crowd onto two streets? Five families were crammed into every small house, all living on top of each other. The Levin family already resided on one of the designated streets, but still, when four other families moved in, life became hard.

"I know what the Germans like best." Alex stood outside his home and looked out onto the crowded street of the ghetto.

"What?" replied Sam, even though he wasn't particularly interested.

"They like to shout and they like rules."

All Jews had to wear a yellow star, front and back. Jews could not leave the ghetto. Jews could not own cows or chickens. Jews were allotted 100 grams of bread, but only if they worked. Children between ten and fifteen years were ordered to sweep the floors of the glass factory. Older boys and men were sent off to do hard labour. It seemed that as each day passed, a new rule or regulation was issued. Alex worked in the glass factory, and Sam did construction on the roads and railways. They were always tired, always hungry, and because water was scarce, they were always dirty too.

In August 1942, when Alex was nine years old, all Jews were ordered to congregate in the market square. Word spread up and down the streets of the ghetto like wildfire. Everyone was upset and confused.

"Go to the market square? My grandmother is too old to walk that distance," said one.

"My wife, she is with child. What about her?" said another.

"My son has a fever. He must not leave his bed," pleaded a mother.

To show that they were *kind* and *tolerant*, the Nazis said that those too old or ill did not have to come to the square.

"But why must we collect in the square in the first place?" The question was on everyone's lips.

"Not to worry," said the SS officers and their collaborators. "The plan is to count all the Jews of Rokitno, that is all. Do not be afraid."

The Jews of Rokitno trekked down to the market square, were counted, and sent back home. But then a few days passed and they were called back to the market a second time and counted again. Why? Anxiety ran high in the once-peaceful town.

The third time they were told to assemble at the market square was different. No one was exempt. The sick, the frail, brand-new mothers, and even those about to give birth were all required to present themselves.

Mama divided up what was left of the family's food. Mama, Papa, Sam, Alex, and Moshe marched down to the square carrying bags and rucksacks. Everyone, including Alex, could feel a tension in the air. Mothers jostled their babies on their hips, fathers paced, grandmothers and grandfathers worried. *What is it that they want? Why are we here?* Words, worries, whispers, fears.

The market square was next to the railroad station, and they could see that there were trains on the tracks. But these weren't passenger trains, they were cattle cars. Why cattle cars? Were the Nazis going to take away their animals? A commander marched up and down, his right hand resting on a gun in his holster. He looked out at the crowd with a scowl.

The Nazis counted everyone, then they shouted, "Women and children to the left, men and boys to the right."

Mama panicked and called out to Alex's father, "No, we must stay together!" The Nazis' dogs snarled and police, drawing their guns, began to surround them. And then a woman screamed, "They are going to kill us!" The frenzy was instant. The crowd rose up in one mighty swell and began to run in every direction. Children were trampled, the old and the handicapped were left behind, people were pushed and shoved, and the German guard dogs were set loose. The shooting began.

"Alex! Alex!" Twice Sam lost sight of his little brother. He bobbed and weaved through the crowd, looking for Alex, and when at last he found him he reached through the throng and grabbed hold of his hand. The two brothers ran, ran as fast as they could.

"What about Mama and Papa and Moshe?" Alex huffed.

"They are together. Father will protect them. Come, I know where to go." Sam was now eleven years old and he took charge. They headed for the railway station and rested for a moment behind the building. Once they'd caught their breath, they ran across the railway tracks and into the bush.

Alex and Sam trudged from one village to another. Occasionally they met others on the run. "What happened at the market?" They asked the question over and over. The answer was always the same. "Some died. Some escaped. The rest were taken away on railway cars."

They passed through village after village. A few people were kind, or at least they were not unkind. Occasionally they were even given food. One day they came upon a farmer in his field. "Do not stay here," he said, looking over his shoulder. "There are Nazi collaborators everywhere. Yesterday they killed five boys with axes."

Was such a thing possible?

By now the boys were starving and exhausted. They slept wherever they found shelter, in haystacks and barns, but always with one eye open, looking out for the Nazis. They begged and stole what they could. But thoughts of Mama, Papa, and Moshe haunted them. What if their parents and little brother had returned home? What if Papa was looking for them?

"We should go home. We should see for ourselves," said Alex, and Sam agreed.

It was past midnight when they crept into Rokitno. "We must wait for daylight," whispered Sam. Finally the sun rose and the village awoke.

"Look!" Alex pointed to a man walking down the street. It was a neighbour. He was carrying a piece of their furniture on his back.

"Why are you here?" another neighbour, a man they had

known all their lives, hissed at the boys as they stood on the road. "You will be killed. Go, go now!"

Alex and Sam were speechless, but they had no doubt that what they'd been told was true. Once again they took to the road.

One day they approached another village; both boys could see the church steeple poking into the clouds. The signpost said "Okopy."

"Look!" Alex sucked in his breath as he pointed to a poster nailed to a post nearby. It said that anyone who turned in a Jew would get a kilogram of salt. Salt? A person could be traded for salt? "Keep walking." Sam prodded his brother on.

"Sam, I can't walk any farther." It had been days since they had eaten anything more than a lump of black bread.

Sam made the decision quickly. "Come on."

They walked up to a house beside the church. Sam tapped on the door. No response. Taking a deep breath he gave the thick wooden door five good thumps.

The door swung open and there, standing on the threshold and wearing a backward collar, was a tall, thin man in a black dress. His pink skin turned pale.

He knows we are Jews, thought Alex. They waited for the man to holler "Police!" or slam the door in their faces, or arrest them himself and march them down to the police station. The boys were ready for anything except what did happen.

The man with the backward collar opened the door wider. "Hurry, hurry." He waved them inside. The door was slammed shut behind them with a thundering thud. The house was cool, almost damp, and smelled of lemon polish.

"Felicja," the man called out. When there was no answer he said, "Wait here," and disappeared down the hall.

"I know what he is," Sam whispered. Alex nodded. He did too. The man was a priest. They had seen priests on the streets of Rokitno, but not up close, and never had either actually spoken to such a man.

The footsteps coming towards them now were fast and furious: *tap, tap, click, click*. The boys were ready to bolt when a large Polish woman, followed by the priest, was upon them.

"Come, boys, quickly," said the woman. She said her name was Felicja Masojada, and the priest's name was Ludwik Wrodarchuk, and for the moment they were the boys' saviours.

"Eat," Felicja said kindly as she refilled Alex's bowl and pushed it under his nose. Sam and Alex grinned. Not only did they have food in their bellies, but they were clean too, and tonight they would sleep in real beds. Alex could almost feel the pillow under his head.

The pounding on the door came while the boys' spoons were still poised in the air and grins plastered across their faces. All four froze as Father Wrodarchuk and Felicja exchanged fearful looks.

"In here." Felicja opened a cupboard door.

It was a poor place to hide. If the house were searched they would be found immediately. Alex and Sam crouched down in the cupboard atop boots and boxes. They could hear Felicja gathering their dishes and in the distance murmurs, but the words were muffled. They waited. Seconds became minutes and minutes, hours, until at last they heard the priest call to them.

"Come out, boys, they are gone."

He stood in the kitchen, looking pale and sorrowful. Alex and Sam climbed out of the closet, all bent and stiff.

"It wasn't the SS," the priest said to Felicja in a low, shaky voice. "It was the police. Someone must have seen the boys come to the door. They have agreed not to search the house today, but they will be back."

No one, the boys thought, especially the local police, would want to arrest the village priest, but the message was clear: harbouring Jews would not be tolerated.

With tears in his eyes, the priest sat on a chair and spoke softly to the boys. "You must go to the forest."

Felicja went off in search of supplies while the priest drew a map and tried his best to caution them of the dangers they might face.

Under cover of darkness, the boys left the priest's home and set off for the forest. But how to live among the trees? Where would they get food? How would they find shelter?

No one had ever taught them the skills they now needed to survive.

It took days to walk into the deepest part of the forest. They crossed streams and climbed steep hills. Winter had not yet set in but the nights were cold. Their feet felt like rocks in their tattered shoes, their noses and ears froze, and their muscles ached, but still they kept going.

"Look." Alex pointed up to a cliff. They saw movement. "Come on."

There were people living in the caves, and they had been watching the boys for some time. They could see that Alex and Sam were on the run, just as they were. There was a three-year-old with her mother and big sister. There was a seven-year-old boy with his mother and sister, and another boy with his mother, all Jewish. Eight people in all … and now there were ten.

"You grab the cow by the nose ring and I'll milk it."

Alex and Sam had become proficient at stealing milk. Breaking a few branches to mark their way back to the caves, they collected milk from cows put out to pasture. They trailed wild pigs that sniffed out underground potatoes. A fire was built in the sand and the potatoes were pushed down deep to bake there.

They cooked over an oak fire. Pine would create too much smoke. They tapped birch trees for sap and gathered mushrooms and berries. Everything was shared.

Shoes were now fashioned out of bark, and socks were made from stolen burlap bags that farmers used to make cheese. The cave-dwellers had become adept at stealing from the farms that surrounded the forest.

Lice were always a problem, but they had a solution for that too. They draped their lice-infested clothes over anthills. Not only did the ants eat the lice but they gobbled up the lice eggs as well.

Months had passed, and all but two of their new friends had survived the winter. The mother and her three-year-old daughter, a baby really, had died of hunger.

Occasionally Alex and Sam made their way back to the village. They were as hungry for information as they were for food. Often, in the far distance, they could hear the sounds of war, bomb blasts mostly. The priest gave them food and news about the progress of the war. Back they went into the forest with small treasures: a few lumps of coal, a tin of meat, some sausage links.

They were used to the hooting of owls and the long, wailing cries of wolves in the distance. Owls were harmless and the wolves never came too near the caves. But it was early spring, the snow was still on the ground, and the wolves were as hungry as the boys were.

One night, the eyes of the wolves glowed yellow in the darkness. Their paws beat the snow as they paced back and forth in front of the caves. The Nazis hunted them in the villages, and wolves stalked them in the forest.

"What should we do?" whispered Alex.

Crouching at the entrance to their cave, Alex and Sam looked out at those gleaming eyes. In the moonlight, Alex's breath made little white puffs as his heart thumped in his ears. Sam tried to quell his own fears and think of a solution.

"The coal!" Alex pulled the precious lumps out of a tin can. With a rock in one hand and the tin held firmly to the ground, the boys made holes in the tin can and looped a bit of rope through the sides. They dropped two glowing coal embers into the tin, then Alex ran out of the cave, screaming and swinging the tin above his head. The wolves scattered. The tin can, a bit of rope, and a glowing ember became part of their survival kit.

"Sam?" Alex lay beside his brother on the rock floor of the cave. "Sam, are you awake?"

Getting information about the war was almost impossible but Alex had an idea. "Sam, I want to join the Partisans." The Partisans were fighting the Nazis. They had seen signs of them over their months in hiding. "We know the forest better than anyone. We could help. We could fight."

Sam rolled over and looked at his little brother. He had been thinking the same thing. They were not the same boys who had run away from the market a year ago. They had lived for a long time now by their wits, seen the very best and the very, very worst in mankind, grown lean and perhaps a little mean too. But could they fight?

They thought of their parents, their little brother, Moshe, the poster that said that a Jewish life was worth a kilogram of salt. Yes, they could fight. It was agreed. They would find the Partisans and ask to join the Resistance. Sam and Alex said their goodbyes and set off.

The Partisans were always on the move, and while their base camp might be anywhere, they often set up close to railways and roads in order to wreak as much havoc as they could on the enemy. It was only when a gun was pointed directly at Alex and Sam that they knew they had reached their destination.

"Where are your guns?" was the first question asked. Neither Sam nor Alex had ever held a gun, let alone fired one. The Partisan grimaced. The boys had good intentions, but good intentions would not win this war. They were told to sit by the fire. "Eat." It seemed like an order.

It was hard to tell who the leader was, but as Alex and Sam

gobbled down the first hot meal they had had in weeks they waited and watched the men deliberate.

"You can stay." The Partisan who had aimed his gun at them was now pointing a finger at Sam. Then he turned to Alex. "But you, you are too small."

The next morning, Alex set out for the cave, alone. Head down, he put one foot in front of another. He must not cry, *of all things, he must not cry*. What would he do without his brother? Worse than hunger and fear was the thought of being alone.

Footsteps! He was being followed. Nazis? Police? Why hadn't he paid attention? Alex threw himself behind a tree and ducked. His heart thumped, his breath caught in his throat. *Please, please* … He made himself small.

"How come you don't walk this fast when we are together?" Sam, looking down, was leaning against a tree.

"Why?" Alex sputtered. "Why did you not stay with them?"

"We are a team. We should stay together." Sam grinned.

Instead of crying Alex smiled. The smile turned into a grin and the grin became a laugh. It had been a long, long time since either boy had laughed out loud.

POSTSCRIPT

Alex and his brother spent a total of eighteen months in the forest. Upon liberation in January 1944 by the Soviets, they walked out of the woods with thirty people who had also been hiding in different caves. Alex was twelve years old and weighed seventy pounds.

Alex became a messenger boy in the Red Army and eventually attended a military cadet school in the Soviet Union. In 1975, he immigrated to Canada, passed the engineering exams, and began his career. Now retired, he has been married to Marina for over fifty years. They have one daughter and two grandchildren.

Sam married Haya and has a son and a daughter and five grandchildren.

Natan, an honoured citizen of Haifa, died in 1994 in Israel. He left two sons, a daughter, and five grandchildren.

Alex's parents, little brother, uncles, and aunts were killed near the city of Sarny, sixty kilometres from Rokitno. Their bodies were tossed into pits along with those of 18,000 other murdered men, women, and children.

The priest Ludwik Wrodarchuk and the Polish teacher Felicja Masojada were murdered during the war by the Nazis and are today listed in Jerusalem as "Righteous Among the Nations"—an honorific bestowed by Israel to recognize non-Jews who acted heroically to save the lives of Jews during the Holocaust.

A poem written by Fred Zolotkovsky, a friend of Alex's from the cadet school in the Soviet Union

These dark woods are our salvation.
Knee-deep in water, but we're alive!
Dreams will save us for life.
Our dugout is the sweetest home.
Only hope that the Germans won't rush here
All at once with a pack of dogs,
That the policeman won't notice with his trained eye
The smoke through the darkness.
We all are worth only a carton of salt.
One kilogram is the price for your whole life:
Your soul, and heart, and blood,
And only because you're a Jew.

MISSION
ACCOMPLISHED

· France, 1943 ·
FÉE BEYTH GOLDFARB'S STORY

Fée as a young woman after the war.

FÉE PICKED UP THE LETTER and read it one more time. "*George is looking for a secretary,*" it said. "*Could you meet with Ernst Appenszeller at a small café outside of Nice?*" Fée turned the letter over in her hands. There was no return address, and no identifying markings.

"What are you going to do?"

Raising her head, Fée gazed at the face of the anxious young woman who had asked the question. Simone was the one in charge here at the chalet in the mountains of France where Fée was working, looking after young boys. But Fée had known Simone long before she'd arrived here. Simone had been her teacher at the Château de la Guette, the first children's home that Fée had lived in after arriving in France from her home in Germany. Simone was older than Fée, who was just eighteen years old, and had always looked out for her—was always there for her. But Simone was a worrier.

"I'm going to go," Fée replied.

"But who is this George person, and how do you know this isn't some kind of trap?"

This time, it was Hannah asking the question. *Hannah worries more than Simone*, thought Fée. But Hannah was also a good friend, and she had been working with Fée here in the chalet for months. She knew that both Hannah and Simone had her best interests at heart.

Fée shrugged her shoulders. "I don't know if it's a trap or not," she said. "And I have no idea who George is, or if he even exists. But I do know Ernst." She went on to remind Simone and Hannah that Ernst Appenszeller had also lived in La Guette. They had been friends during that time, and now this friend was reaching out to her in some way. Fée needed to respond.

"I think this note might be Ernst's way of getting me to come meet him without giving away too much information," continued Fée.

These days, notes could easily fall into the hands of the wrong people. Nazis were always on the lookout for Jews, like Fée and her friends. Ordinary citizens might willingly betray their Jewish neighbours. The note that Fée held in her hands said little, but it instructed her to get on a train in the nearby town of Digne heading towards the city of Nice. She was to get off two stops before reaching Nice and meet Ernst in a designated café. There was nothing more in the note.

"Besides," Fée added, smiling at Hannah, "I'm curious about it. Wouldn't you be, in my shoes?"

"No!" said Hannah. "Meddling in other people's affairs is going to get you into trouble. I think we're very lucky to be here in this safe place. We need to stay put. Why would you ever take this chance and go marching off into what might be a very dangerous situation?"

Fée looked away. *I'm not like Hannah*, she thought. Was she nosy, as Hannah had suggested? She didn't think so. She didn't concern herself with other people's business unless she was invited. But she *was* daring.

"*You* understand, don't you, Simone?" Fée asked. "*You* know why I have to do this."

Simone sighed and shook her head. "Just promise me that you won't go into the city," she said. "Stay out of Nice."

The city of Nice, on the southeast coast of France, was already occupied by Italian forces, and Italy was a strong ally of Hitler and his Nazi armies. As dangerous as it was to travel in the countryside, it was even more risky to enter the city, where soldiers patrolled the streets, looking to arrest Jews.

"I promise," Fée replied as she turned to go. "Don't worry, Hannah," she added, squeezing her friend's hand. "I'll be back soon."

Fée spotted Ernst as soon as she got off the train. It was good to see her old friend.

"I want you to come with me to Nice," Ernst said, after they had greeted one another. "I want you to meet Henri Pohoryles. Remember him? He was a teacher with us at La Guette. It's important, or I wouldn't ask you," Ernst added.

Fée paused, mindful of Simone's warning and her own promise to stay out of Nice. *But what harm is there in going?* she wondered. *After all, Ernst will be there to look after me. And this invitation is becoming more interesting by the minute.* Fée nodded. She would go with Ernst to Nice, have the meeting with Henri, and take the train back to the chalet. Nothing would go wrong. And Simone would never know.

The train ride to Nice was uneventful, just as Fée had predicted. And before long, she found herself in a small hotel room, facing Henri and listening with interest to his proposal.

"We want you to join the Resistance," Henri announced. "We are part of a group called the AJS, the Armée Juifs Secret, also known as the Underground Jewish Army. We are working with other Jews, helping them to stay safe during these difficult times. You are just the kind of person we need as part of our organization."

Fée shivered and reached up to adjust her round, dark-rimmed glasses. The room was cold, and her old winter jacket did little to keep her warm. Her mother had bought the coat for her in 1939, when Fée was only fifteen years old. It barely fit, but it was one of her few possessions from home and she did not want to part with it. Fée pulled the collar up close to her ears as she thought about what Henri was saying. She had heard about this group, the AJS. She knew there were groups of Resistance fighters in and around the cities of France, and other countries as well. Even though she knew their work was dangerous, she was curious about how she could be involved.

"There are Resistance groups that are fighting with weapons in the forests and mountains," Henri continued. "They are blowing up munitions factories and sabotaging the trains—anything to slow down the progress of Hitler and his armies. Our group, the AJS, doesn't carry arms, but our fight is just as important."

Ernst nodded and picked up the story. "We are here to help our Jewish brothers and sisters, those who are hiding from the Nazis or trying to get out of France. We forge documents for them, we smuggle food, and we find safe hiding places. We bring them clothing and whatever else they need to survive, and to remain out of the hands of our enemies."

"I know you are smart and resourceful," added Henri. "You would be a tremendous help to our organization. Will you join us?"

Fée wasted no time in replying. "Yes!" she nearly shouted out loud. This was just what she was looking for—a way to help other Jews, a way to feel useful. She *was* smart, it was true. And she would put her ingenuity and cunning to good use.

There in the quiet and cold of the stark hotel room, Fée was sworn in as a member of the AJS.

"I swear allegiance to the cause of the AJS," she repeated solemnly after Henri. "I will carry out my missions without question, and I will work to protect Jews in need."

Henri nodded and pulled a document out of his pocket. "Here," he said. "It's a new identity card."

Fée took the card and stared down at the name printed on it. From now on, her name would no longer be Erika Felicitas Beyth. From now on, she would be known as Alise Raynal.

"Make the card look worn," Ernst added. "Right now, it's too new and clean. Rub it on the ground, walk on it—

anything to make it look like you've had it for years. And here is some money." He handed some bills over to Fée. "Go back to the chalet and get your things. Then go to the post office in Lyon. Your first orders will be waiting for you there."

The three young comrades shook hands. "Welcome to our organization," said Henri, and then he and Ernst were gone.

Simone was waiting for Fée when she returned to the chalet. She took one look at her young friend and said, "You're leaving, aren't you?"

Fée nodded.

"I'm not surprised," said Simone. "I knew this was going to happen … They are lucky to have you," she added.

Hannah did not take the news quite so easily. "Why are you doing this?" she cried, as she and Fée sat in their room that night. "Don't you realize how dangerous this is? You could be arrested. You could be killed!"

Fée took her friend's hand and smiled gently. "I'm doing what I've been asked to do," she said. "I don't ask questions. I just know that I need to find a way to be useful, and this is it."

Hannah looked down. "You're braver than I am," she said softly.

"No," Fée replied firmly. "You could do this too, Hannah."

"But no one asked *me* to join the Resistance," said Hannah, wisely. "They've asked you. They see something in you that I don't have—that others don't have. You're the one they chose, and you know there's a reason for that."

Fée didn't respond. She knew there was truth in what Hannah was saying. Fée *was* different, less fearful than others, and more confident. The fact was if she had been a more timid person, she would never have agreed to this assignment, and the AJS would never have asked her to join. Fée could not admit this to Hannah, though. Instead, she asked, "Will you do something for me?"

Hannah nodded.

"I need you to keep this safe." Fée held out a small metal box. She opened it and touched the personal possessions inside: her real birth certificate, a few photographs, letters— unimportant to anyone but her. Then she closed the box and handed it to Hannah. "It's all I have, and I won't be able to take it with me."

Hannah nodded again. "I'll bury it on the mountainside, so no one will ever get it. You never know what might happen to us here," she added.

Early the next morning, Fée found herself on a train heading for the city of Lyon and her first assignment. Ernst had said to go to the post office, and she had no difficulty finding it near the train station after she had disembarked. Fée entered the old building and walked towards the letterboxes. She stared straight ahead and walked with purpose, hardly hesitating, knowing she had to look as though she knew what she was doing. Soldiers walked past with their rifles casually slung over their shoulders. Fée ignored them. She was not afraid.

She stopped in front of the wall of letterboxes and reached into her coat pocket, withdrawing a small key. Reaching up, she ran her fingers over the numbers that labelled each box, searching for the one that Ernst had told her to memorize. Finally, her fingers settled on the last box in the second row. She inserted the key, opened the small door, and removed a plain brown envelope. Glancing quickly over her shoulder, Fée opened the envelope and read the instructions.

Go to the marketplace in Lyon and meet your contact at the small fountain. He will carry a dark brown suitcase that he will give to you. Take the suitcase and board the train for Toulouse.

The letter went on to instruct Fée to take the suitcase to a small bookstore in Toulouse. There she would meet with Tante Walter, who ran the bookstore. She would leave the suitcase with Tante Walter and return to Lyon.

Fée reached into the envelope once more and withdrew the money that had been left for her to purchase her train ticket. The Resistance had planned everything. They were well organized, down to the last detail. Briefly, she wondered where the money came from, but she quickly pushed the thought from her mind. *No questions*, she whispered to herself. *Just carry out the mission.*

As soon as she entered the marketplace, Fée spotted the designated fountain, along with her contact, a small, pleasant-looking man with a grey overcoat and cap. He smiled, shook hands with Fée, and handed her the suitcase as instructed. He didn't speak, simply touched his fingers to his forehead in a casual salute before turning to walk quickly away. Before Fée had a chance to return the nod, the man had disappeared into the crowd. Fée made her way back to the train station, clutching the suitcase.

"One ticket for Toulouse," she said, approaching the ticket counter and leaning forward to be heard through the iron bars that separated the passengers from the ticket agents. She held the money out in front of her.

"I'll issue the ticket," the man behind the counter said, "but there's no train tonight. Another one of the bridges between here and Toulouse is out. There are only a few trains getting through."

Fée's heart sank. This news was a mixed blessing. On the one hand, she knew that the Allies were bombing bridges in France in an attempt to isolate Hitler's armies and prevent them from moving equipment and soldiers through the country. On the other hand, Fée could not begin to imagine how this interruption in her plan might affect her mission to Toulouse.

"When will the train leave?" she asked, still clutching the suitcase in her other hand.

The man shrugged. He looked bored, as if he had been answering this question too many times from too many distraught passengers. "In a few hours, if you're lucky … early tomorrow at the worst. I wouldn't go too far from the station," he added, sliding the ticket under the bars towards Fée. "Next person in line!"

Slowly, Fée moved away from the counter and looked around. *Now what?* she wondered, before sinking down onto a hard wooden bench. She pulled the suitcase up onto her lap, resisting the urge to click open the latches and look inside.

The man at the counter had said not to go too far. That meant only one thing: Fée would have to spend the night here in the station and get on the first train leaving in the morning. She opened her coat and leaned her head forward to rest on the suitcase. Wrapping her arms around it, Fée took the first deep breath she had taken since this mission began. Up until now, she had been operating on automatic, going where she was instructed, doing the things she had been told to do. There had been no time to pause or think. You had to stay sharp in this espionage business, Fée realized. Plans could change in a flash, and there was no one

to turn to. She had only herself. *Maybe it's better to be alone,*
Fée thought. No one to turn to meant no one to worry
about. Fée had been on her own for years, ever since the
beginning of the war, when her parents had sent her from
her home in Germany to France for her safekeeping. She
didn't know where they were, or if they were still alive. She
didn't know what had become of her older brother. The
news that sometimes reached her from Germany was not
good, especially for Jews. Fée shook her head, pushing these
thoughts away. *I wonder what Hannah is doing right now,* she
thought briefly, before closing her eyes and drifting off to
sleep.

"Attention!" The loudspeaker blared through the train
station, waking Fée with a start. She blinked and sat up,
stretching painfully and moving her neck in a slow circle.
How long had she slept—an hour, maybe two? The voice on
the loudspeaker continued to blast, announcing the departure of the train to Toulouse.

Quickly, Fée grabbed the precious suitcase, stood up, and
joined the line of passengers trying to board the train. She
had not been the only one to sleep in the station. Hundreds
of people were there with her, pushing and shoving, trying to
get on board, knowing that there might not be another train
for days. Fée was determined not to be left behind. She
gritted her teeth and inched her way forward until she finally
climbed the steep stairs onto the train and entered the

compartment. It was packed. There was no hope of getting a seat. But that wasn't the worst of Fée's problems.

"You can't hold on to the suitcase," a man next to Fée ordered. "There's barely enough room for the people."

"Put it on the rack above the seats," a woman said. "You'll get it back when we get to Toulouse."

Fée shook her head and clutched the suitcase closer to her body. "No, I … I … I need it … I need to k-keep it," she stuttered.

"What's the matter with you?" the woman replied. "Don't be a fool. Just put your case on the rack. It's crowded enough in here without the bags."

Others around Fée were beginning to notice the commotion. There was too much attention being paid to her, and finally, Fée had no choice but to surrender her case. She watched helplessly as a man lifted it up onto the luggage rack. Then, as more and more people boarded the train, Fée was pushed and jostled farther and farther away from her suitcase.

The crowd continued to shove until Fée found herself being pushed into one of the small toilets. Five people were already inside, jammed together in the tiny space, and as if a tidal wave had pushed from behind, Fée was thrown up against them. She could barely breathe.

Finally, the whistle blew, and the train began to inch its way out of the station. Fée stretched her neck, trying to peer around the corner of the toilet to see the case.

"Excuse me," she whispered to the woman next to her. "Would you exchange spots with me, please? I just need to get close to those seats over there."

"I'm not going anywhere, and neither are you," the woman replied. "What's the urgency? Two hours, three with all the stops, and we'll be in Toulouse. Then you'll get your stuff back."

Three hours! That was bad enough. But it was the thought of the train stopping along the way that made Fée shudder. There was always the danger that Nazi soldiers would board the train at each stop, inspecting the cars and asking for papers. Fée had her false documents, so that would be no problem. But if there were an inspection, passengers would have to claim their luggage. After the fuss she had made about relinquishing it, too many people in the train car already knew that she was the owner of the brown suitcase. Fée would have no choice but to admit that the case was hers. And for the first time since beginning this mission, the thought of claiming the suitcase terrified Fée.

What's inside that case? she wondered. *Is it equipment to make bombs? Could it be money, or guns?* She had no idea, but she knew she had to be carrying something of value, something possibly dangerous, and something that was illegal.

The next three hours were agonizing for Fée. Each time the train stopped, she held her breath, waiting to see if soldiers would come on board. Her mind raced with thoughts of arrest and possible deportation to prison or a concentration camp. By the time the train arrived in Toulouse, Fée was exhausted with anxiety and weak with relief. But her mission was not yet over. She pushed her way through the passenger car, grabbed the suitcase, descended from the train, and began to make her way to the bookstore, her predetermined drop-off point.

When Fée pushed open the door to the small bookstore, a bell above the door chimed a soft greeting. A small woman looked up as Fée entered. She glanced at the suitcase in Fée's hand and smiled.

"We've been expecting you," the woman said.

"Tante Walter?" asked Fée.

The woman nodded. "I assume you had no trouble."

Fée shook her head. She didn't need to explain what she had gone through to get here. The important thing was that she had made it safely, with the suitcase in hand, and without being followed.

"Good! Come with me to the back." With that, Tante Walter pulled open a curtain and gestured for Fée to follow her into the back of the store.

Fée watched in amazement as Tante Walter pushed aside a large bookshelf and slipped behind it. The bookstore in front was merely a cover. In the back, the AJS had set up a secret location to receive shipments like the one Fée carried in her suitcase. Two men sat in this back room, working over some papers. They glanced up as Fée and Tante Walter entered, and then they returned to their work.

Tante Walter pulled the suitcase up onto a table and clicked the latches open. Fée stepped forward as she opened the case to reveal the contents.

"They're electronic transmitters for radios," Tante Walter said, before Fée could ask. "Very important. We'll distribute them to our contacts around the country. Good job," she added, before closing the case and escorting Fée back to the front of the store and out the door.

Fée paused on the streets of Toulouse and took one more deep breath. Mission accomplished. She had served the AJS, done what they had asked of her, and done her job well, though in the future she resolved to ask for more information about what she was carrying from location to location. For the moment, that didn't matter. Fée felt proud, and satisfied. *That's one mission down*, she thought to herself, and nodded confidently before turning to walk back to the train station.

POSTSCRIPT

Fée continued to run missions for the AJS until the end of the war. Once, she was arrested by the French military police and taken to prison for six weeks. Fortunately, she was released. She was in Lyon when the war ended. Some time later, Fée was honoured with the Croix de Guerre, a medal for her bravery as part of the Jewish Resistance in France.

Fée married Eric Goldfarb in 1947. He had also survived the war as a member of the Resistance. Eric and Fée came to Canada in 1952. Fée has three children and four grandchildren.

TWO ON THE ROAD

• Trawna Labour Camp, Poland, 1943 •

SALLY (SARAH) BARATH EISNER'S STORY

*Sally, age 7, with brother Abe, age 3,
and their mother, Yeta Ett, in Poland, 1932.*

"SALLY, IS THAT YOUR FATHER?" Donia pointed to a dark figure making long strides towards them.

Sally squinted. It was hard to tell. And then, "Oh, Daddy, no. Go back. Go back!" Where were the guards? Her eyes darted to the four corners of the field. What was he thinking? He should not have been out in the fields like this!

Every day, girls were marched from Trawna Labour Camp to work in the fields. It was July, and the corn crop was miserably sparse, although not from lack of effort. The tools the girls used were clumsy, rusted, and often damaged. Many girls dug trenches with split hoes while others knelt down on scabby knees, stabbing the earth with broken shovels. The farm machinery that might have tilled the soil and planted the crops had long since been taken away to help farmers elsewhere—maybe the German farmers of the Fatherland.

Sally shielded her eyes from the sun. The air was prickly and the heat of the July day felt like a flat hand pressing down on the earth. There were no guards in sight, but that didn't mean that one might not suddenly appear. The Germans were in control of the area and the camp, but these guards were ordinary field hands. Some were just boys who were willing to do whatever the Nazis told them, while others were bullies who enjoyed their newfound power. None, however, was harmless. If they caught her father, they would march him back to the camp and turn him over to the commandant.

"Daddy, what are you doing?" Sally whispered as her father came closer.

"You did not eat this morning." Sally's father—tall, gaunt, with piercing blue eyes looking out from a handsome face— reached into his pocket and pulled out a potato.

"Get down, Daddy!" She yanked on her father's sleeve and the two crouched among the cornstalks. "You must go back! Please, go back!" Why had he put himself at such risk? Tears welled up in her eyes. This was madness … but then, it was all madness.

"It will be your birthday in a few days." Her father smiled as he slipped the potato into Sally's hand. "It is not the gift that I thought I would give my only daughter on her sixteenth birthday." His smile was sad; it wasn't a smile at all, really.

"Go, Daddy, please."

He nodded, and left her there among the corn and the dirt.

"Daddy?" She watched as he grew smaller and smaller in the distance until he disappeared altogether. "Thank you," she whispered, although by now he was much too far away to hear.

"Sally, get to work," Donia hissed.

Sally didn't need to look around to know that she was being watched. With a practised jab she stuck her hoe into the ground and turned the earth.

Why had her father taken such a chance? Life in the labour camp was terrible—worse than terrible. There were no food rations, and what they ate they stole. But they were so much better off than most of the people there. Sally's father worked as a bookkeeper in the camp office and Mama in the kitchen. And Sally's twelve-year-old brother Abe tended to the horses. They were lucky because they were together. They had much to lose.

Sally touched the potato in her pocket. She wouldn't eat it. She would take it back to the camp tonight and share it with her family. ·

"Listen." Donia cocked her ear to the wind.

Sally leaned on her hoe and listened. "It's thunder."

"No, not thunder," said Donia. "Guns. I hear guns."

All the girls in the field stopped to listen. They heard the rattle of bullets being spit out of a machine gun, then single shots as well.

"Russians," called out a girl down the line.

"Maybe Americans," cried one of the younger girls.

"No, listen. I hear crying."

"That was a scream. I'm sure of it."

"Why would people scream if the Americans had arrived?"

No one had an answer to that.

The distant shooting went on for some time and then … nothing. A half-hour passed and the noise started up again, but this time it was coming from behind them. All the while, heavy clouds were gathering as the sky grew darker and darker, and there were rumbles in the distance too. First came a flash of lightning followed by repeated claps of thunder, and then a downpour. The sounds of gunfire stopped.

A guard began to yell commands at the girls, but his words were lost as the heavy rain began. At first the rain felt good. It was warm and washed away weeks and weeks of grime, but soon it turned into a torrent. It pelted the skin and drenched the field. The sky turned black.

"It's like the end of the world!" cried one of the girls. The next clap of thunder was so loud that many girls threw down their hoes and shovels and began to run back to the camp.

"Stop!" the guards shouted. Then another clap of thunder sent the young guards running too.

Sally stayed alone in the field among the cornstalks. She sat on her haunches and made herself small, as small as she could. It was July 1943. There were rumours that the war had turned, that Hitler and his evil army would soon be beaten. Could it be true? But she'd heard screaming. Why?

Night came on and still she didn't move. Once in a while she gnawed at the potato, then she chided herself for being so greedy. She must share it with her parents and her little brother. Still, she waited. Maybe she should go back to the camp now. Maybe not. Trust her instincts, that's what she should do. The rain had stopped but she was soaked and so cold.

By the time dawn broke she knew that she had to go back. Hungry, tired, and sodden, Sally left the field and stumbled back to the camp.

There were guards in the guard tower but nothing seemed right. The gates lay open, and inside the camp people milled around, confused and traumatized.

"Sally, where were you? We thought you were dead." One of the girls from the fields came running towards her. "Sally!" The girl shook her arm. "Your parents, they are gone."

Gone? Gone where? Sally gazed into the girl's face. She was a Gentile girl, Polish. There were lots of peasant girls who worked in the labour camps, and most were treated no better than the Jewish girls.

"It was an *aktion*. They marched them into the woods and ..." Her voice trailed away.

No, no. Not Mama, not Daddy. Dead? Not possible. Sally couldn't breathe. Her parents were good, gentle people. Why did the Germans say that her parents were worthless because they were Jewish? Why did they make up lies about people? These Nazis were murderers, all of them. And then—Abe!

"Have you seen my brother? Has anyone seen my brother? Oh please, God, no." Air wasn't getting into her lungs. She spun in different directions; the world swirled around and around and around and around. Had they killed Abe too?

"I saw him." Another Polish girl, with a round, flat face and hair the colour of corn, stepped forward. "He ran into the woods. I think he wanted to see if your parents were really dead."

"Where?" Sally steadied herself and drew in a long breath. "Which direction?"

The girl pointed. "But you can't go. You'll be shot."

Shot? Let them shoot her. What did it matter? Her parents were dead, her home was gone, and now her brother was likely dead too. Let them kill her. Dying had to be easier than living like this.

It wasn't hard to follow the trail made by several hundred people as they were marched to their deaths. The ground was soft from the rain and most of the footprints had been washed away, but she could make out a few on the grassy banks of the path. Did they belong to her parents? *Mama, were you scared? Daddy, were you worried about Abe and me?*

She didn't have to walk far before coming up to a stand of trees and long rows of trenches. There were curious pools of dark water everywhere: blood and rain mixed together in the mud.

Sally stood on the lip of a long trench. *Are you in there, Daddy? Mama, can you hear me?* The trenches were filled with dirt. Sally crumpled to the ground. *I'll not forget this day, I promise. And if I live, I'll tell people about you. I'll tell anyone who will listen, and I'll tell those who won't listen too.*

Abe, where was he? Abe loved horses. If he was still alive, Sally knew where to look.

It wasn't a long walk or even a hard one, but putting one foot in front of the other took every ounce of strength Sally had. And there he was.

"Abe, Abe!"

She ran, ran as if her legs were wings. For the very briefest of seconds, the smallest of moments, there was a relief so intense, a joy so overwhelming that she was transported back to a time when happiness was possible.

Abe sat, dry-eyed, under a tree, in the open, for anyone to see—a Nazi, a policeman, a collaborator, a soldier. Below him was the horse pasture.

"Abe?" Sally reached for his hand. He didn't say anything. "Abe?"

He looked up at her with blank eyes. Sally reached out. He stood, took her hand, and they started to walk.

They came upon six or seven cottages gathered at a bend in the road. From a distance the homes looked like eggs in a nest, all cozy and warm. Here people ate dinner, went about their work, sent their children to school—and not more than a few kilometres away, people were being murdered.

Slowly, Sally and Abe approached the hamlet. Up close, the homes were neither charming nor pretty. Many cottages had ragged thatched roofs with untended, broken fences, and the poultry yards were filthy. Sally's heart began to thump. What now?

"Sally, I'm hungry," whispered Abe.

They were both hungry. Her decision was made quickly. "Come."

They walked up to the first cottage and knocked at the door. A woman answered. The shock on her face was enough to make Sally peer down at her clothes. Her dress, torn and splattered with mud, hung off her spindly frame in shreds. She could feel her bones poking through her skin. At just sixteen years of age she felt like a very old woman. She looked at her little brother with fresh eyes. Abe looked no better.

The woman hastily crossed herself—*Father, Son, and Holy Spirit*—and motioned with her hand, "Come, come."

The children stumbled into the dark cottage as the woman peered out into the road. Was it possible that no one had seen them? She closed the door, and in the dim light she gazed down at the two waifs. Her name was Mrs. Danicka, she said. Sally and Abe had inadvertently stumbled upon a woman with a heart of gold.

The summer months went by. At Mrs. Danicka's home, the children hid themselves as best they could, but there was no fooling all the neighbours. It was October when Mrs. Danicka, with wet eyes and shaking hands, said, "My neighbours are spying on us. They know. You will be hurt. Run, children." She sobbed as Sally and Abe once again set out on the road.

Days later, they came upon another village, and once again they knocked on a door. A woman with a small baby in her arms answered.

"We can work," Sally said bravely.

The woman eyed the two. Mrs. Danicka had fed them as best she could. While still thin, they were not as haggard and gaunt as they had once been. Besides, Sally had blond hair, and the boy *looked* Aryan enough. They could pass.

"Come in," said the woman, as she shifted her baby from one hip to the other.

Sally was startled. Was it possible that God, who had forsaken their parents, was protecting them for a second time?

The Polish peasants' cottage was one large room. It harboured a stove, some rickety furniture, and a huge bed with a lumpy straw mattress that could sleep maybe eight or nine people. Under the bed were all sorts of things—boots, pots, shovels. There was no fear of rats getting in there. Where would they fit?

"You can't sleep in the house," the young mother announced. "But there is an open shed full of hay in the yard. You can sleep in it." She looked at Sally. "You can help by taking care of the baby during the day. As for the boy," she looked down at Abe, "there will be plenty of chores for him to do."

It was a good place. Not warm and welcoming like Mrs. Danicka's home, but there was food, and the young woman and her husband did not mistreat them.

Every night Sally and Abe burrowed into the hay, closed their eyes, and thought of Mama and Daddy. *We're still here. We're still alive.*

Every morning Sally and Abe woke, tired and stiff, to begin their workday. There were no books, no time for

•

learning, no time to think or talk, either. But what was there to think about? There was only survival.

It was December and it was starting to snow. Sally stood by the window peeling root vegetables for dinner. The baby was in her cradle making the mewing sounds babies make when they are beginning to feel hungry. Sally peered into the fading light. There was something in the distance, something odd. Figures on horseback were coming down the road towards them at a gallop. Soldiers? No, worse than soldiers. She could make out the shape of their hats and, as they got a little closer, their uniforms. They were SS!

"Abe, Abe!" Sally flung open the door and grabbed her brother by the neck.

"What is it?" Abe could barely form the question before Sally shoved him under the giant bed.

"Up, up, crawl against the wall!" Her screams alarmed the baby, who started to fuss.

Abe scrambled over boots, kettles, spades, cartons, and wooden boxes—there was no end to the stuff that had collected under this gigantic bed.

Sally looked back at the baby, who was crying in fits and stops. If she could just settle her down. There was a thundering of hooves as the horses drew up to the door.

"Sally," Abe whispered.

She dove under the bed and began to crawl. Bits of unidentifiable metal scraped her skin. She could hear her brother breathing and crawled in the dark towards the sound. And then another miracle. The baby's crying turned into bawling. Her howls were so loud that they reverberated around the room. Any sounds Sally and Abe might have made clambering over the muddle under the bed were masked by the baby's wails.

The SS burst into the house, shouting, "We know there are Jews here!" They toppled furniture. Still the baby screamed. "Where's the brat's mother?" They were speaking German.

Sally held her breath and tried to still her heart. Surely they could hear it pounding in her chest!

"Look! Proof!" a soldier shouted victoriously.

What proof? Sally's mind was frozen. Her breaths were shallow and measured. She stifled a cough.

Bayonets pierced the hay-stuffed mattress over their heads. One sword shot through the straw mattress and grazed Sally's leg. *I won't scream. I won't cry out. Not even if they stab me through the heart.* Abe let out a yelp and Sally covered his mouth with her hand.

Their search had not turned up the Jewish children. At first there was a quarrel among the Nazis about what to do next. Sick of the baby's wailing, one soldier bellowed, "Where are the brat's parents? We'll teach them to harbour Jews."

The search for the baby's parents proved equally fruitless. The SS men hollered to the neighbours, who stood outside lurking in their own doorways, "We'll be back. We know that there are Jews here. We'll be back."

Three grown men with horses, weapons, and power—why were they threatened by two small, starving children? How was it possible? What kind of men were they? Sally knew better than to think this way. It didn't help.

It was at least an hour later when the man and woman returned. By then, the baby's howls had left her exhausted and she slept.

Sally and Abe hadn't moved, not an inch. They heard the man and woman enter, and a few neighbours, besides. Still, they waited under the bed, and when everyone else had left they heard the man and woman talking.

"Where have they gone?"

Slowly, Sally and Abe crawled out. If the Devil himself had emerged from under their bed, the young couple could not have looked more horrified.

"Look, look what you did!" The woman held up little booties, bibs, and a sweater that Sally had crocheted for the baby. It was not the work of a Polish peasant woman—everyone could see that, including the SS men. That was the proof the soldiers had found.

"You must go, now." The woman rocked the baby frantically in her arms.

Now? But it was night, and it was cold, and they had no clothes.

The woman opened the door. And so the two children again walked out into a bitter night.

"Abe, we won't survive out here. We have to go back to the camp. We have no choice."

And so, still holding each other's hands, Sally and Abe walked back into the labour camp.

POSTSCRIPT

Sally and her brother, Abraham, ended up in Tluste, a labour camp. They survived and were liberated by the Soviets in March 1944. Sally married a man she had fallen in love with before the war, Leon Eisner, who himself had survived in the Polish army, then in the Soviet army, and finally in a prisoner-of-war camp under the Nazis. Leon died in 2005.

Sally remains an active volunteer and has a son and a daughter, seven grandchildren, and two great-grandchildren.

CROSSING INTO FREEDOM

· France, 1944 ·

INGE ROSENTHAL SPITZ'S STORY

Left: *Inge at age 12, in 1939, just before she left Germany for France.*
Right: *Inge's sister, Edith, at age 10.*

"GET ON," THE MAN ORDERED. "And don't talk."

The children moved quickly, filing on board the bus that was to take them to freedom.

"Hurry, everyone," Inge whispered, trying to calm the beating of her own heart. At the age of sixteen, Inge was the oldest of the ten who had gathered, and the one in charge. She smiled as her sister, Edith, boarded the bus, and squeezed her hand. "Don't look so worried, Edith. We'll be fine." If only Inge felt as confident as she sounded.

Inge glanced over at the man who was giving the commands. He was to be their *passeur*, their guide. He was tall and thin, and he nervously smoked a cigarette, checking his watch and glancing over his shoulder while scratching at the thick stubble on his chin. Inge didn't know his name; better not to know too much. All she knew was that he was a French smuggler being paid to take the children to the border between France and Switzerland. He would help them get across, and hopefully keep them from falling into the hands of the Nazis who were patrolling in this region, looking for Jews who were trying to escape, just like them. The children were putting their safety, their lives, in the hands of this stranger. Could they trust him? Inge wondered. Then she shook her head and turned back to the children. What choice did they have?

Fourteen-year-old Henri boarded the bus next, followed by Eddie, aged fifteen, and then the other children. The last to climb the stairs was the youngest, a three-year-old boy. Inge smiled fondly at the child. He was so quiet, he wouldn't even tell her his name. Inge called him "Canari" because he wore a bright-yellow jacket and looked like a little yellow bird.

"*Vite*, Canari," Inge whispered in French. "Quickly!" She reached for his arm and helped him up the steep steps of the bus. *How young he is*, Inge thought. *How young all of us are.*

Canari gave Inge a grateful smile. His eyes were red and tired. No one had slept much the night before. In fact, all the children looked as if they might fall down from exhaustion.

They had spent the night sitting on hard wooden benches in the school, waiting for word of their departure. Inge had put her head down on the desk in front of her and closed her eyes, trying to sleep, but it was impossible. Her head was spinning with fear and uncertainty. "If no one comes by 7:00 A.M., then you must go to the post office and receive new orders." That's what the woman had told her, the one who had appeared in Lyon with food coupons for the children. Inge didn't know her name, either. No one had names, and the less you asked about them, the better. This woman was part of a chain of nameless people, all members of the Underground, all helping Inge and the others get away. These mysterious people arranged payment for the *passeur*, and passed on detailed orders about what to do and where to go. *Walk here and receive directions. Then go there and get new directions.* It was like being on an elaborate treasure hunt where the prize at the end was freedom. Inge knew that they had to follow each instruction carefully or risk being captured.

All night long, the children had sat and waited, counting the minutes until the sun would creep up and over the horizon and stream through the school window. At seven o'clock on the dot, Inge heard footsteps in the hallway. She sat up and instinctively pulled Edith closer to her, wrapping her arms around her young sister. And then, a new nameless woman appeared in the classroom, and Inge stood up as she entered. "It's okay," the woman said. "You're leaving." And that was how the ten of them found themselves here on this bus.

"We're ready, monsieur," Inge said, when all the children were settled. The man nodded, and the bus pulled away from the city of Lyon. In three hours, they would be in the town of Annemasse. And then, if everything went according to plan, they would be smuggled across the border from France into Switzerland and they would be free. But a million things could go wrong between now and then. They might be stopped and arrested by the Gestapo, who regularly patrolled these roads. This *passeur* might keep the money he had been given and turn the children over to the authorities. Maybe Switzerland wouldn't agree to take them and would send them back to France. France was already under the control of Adolf Hitler and his Nazi armies. That was why Inge and the others had to escape. So far, Switzerland had managed to remain neutral, but there were reports that even Switzerland was turning refugees back at its borders, particularly Jewish refugees.

Inge could not stop the bad thoughts from rushing through her mind. But she wouldn't let the others see her fear. She was the oldest. She was in charge. They looked to her to be brave and calm, and she could not let them down, no matter how she felt.

Three hours seemed like such a long time, Inge thought, as she turned to stare out the window. But it was nothing compared to the years that Inge and Edith had already spent moving from place to place, hiding who they were, wondering if they would ever see their parents again. Memories flashed like photographs in Inge's mind, and she labelled them with dates and names, as if she were gluing them into a photo album.

November 10, 1938: This snapshot was called Kristallnacht. People called it "The Night of Broken Glass" because the streets of Germany were covered in shattered glass from the windows of shops and homes that were ransacked and from the synagogues that were set on fire. It was also the night that Inge's Papa was arrested.

March 15, 1939: This was Inge's twelfth birthday. Mutti, her mother, tried to pretend that everything was fine. She even baked a chocolate marble cake for the celebration. Uncle Sigfried, Aunt Edith, and her cousin Susan came to celebrate. But her friend Gisella wasn't allowed to come. None of her Christian friends were allowed to talk to Inge any more, just because she was Jewish.

March 20, 1939: The day Inge left home. Mutti said, "Inge, you and Edith are going to France. It's the safest place for you. Inge, you will have to watch the little one," she added, pointing to Edith. Inge nodded, knowing she would have to take care of herself and her sister from then on. She and Edith packed their small suitcases and boarded the train that left Germany far behind. Overnight it took them to a children's home at the Château de la Guette, France. Inge had not seen her Mutti since then.

March 20, 1943: The Gestapo was searching for sixteen-year-old Jewish children in France. Those who were found were being sent to concentration camps, and who knew what would happen after that? Inge was smuggled to a convent and given a new name. She was no longer Ingeborg Dorothea Regina Rosenthal. Now she was Yvette Romer, a French Protestant refugee from Alsace-Lorraine. Inge had learned French, and she spoke it with the ease of a native. She felt French. But when she knelt in the chapel, crossed herself, and said the rosary, her heart always remained Jewish.

May 1, 1943: Mother Superior at the convent asked Inge if she would like to be a maid in a French family. And so, she began to work for Monsieur and Madame Vanvert and their children, François and Jeanette. For one year, Inge cooked, cleaned house, and played with the children, whom she grew to love, all the time pretending to be Yvette Romer, always hiding her Jewish identity, even from the Vanverts.

The night before she left the Vanvert home to begin this flight to Switzerland, Inge gave François a small wooden pencil box. It was one of the few possessions she had kept from home. "I'll miss you most of all, François," Inge said as she handed him the gift and hugged him tightly.

"Why must you go, Yvette?" François cried. "Don't you love us any more?"

How could Inge begin to explain to this little boy that her safety was at stake, and his, if anyone were to find out that she was Jewish. He didn't care about her religion.

If only grown-ups were as kind and trusting as children, Inge thought as she knelt in front of François and looked into his innocent eyes. "I do love you," she said. "Keep this gift and remember me always."

Later that night, Monsieur Vanvert had appeared at her bedroom door, holding the pencil box and looking visibly shaken. "Look at this, Yvette," he said, sliding the wooden top off the box and turning it over. There, in black ink, was Inge's name—not the false name that she had been given to hide her identity as a Jew, but her real name, Inge Rosenthal.

Inge gasped, and looked up into Monsieur Vanvert's black eyes.

"I know who you are," he said. "I know what you are. Do you realize what could happen to my family if you were discovered here?" he demanded.

"Monsieur, I'm so sorry! I didn't realize … I never meant to harm … What will you do?" These last words were whispered hoarsely, as Inge stared at this man.

A minute passed—an eternity. And then, Monsieur Vanvert turned to go. "We will not betray you," he said over his shoulder.

Inge left the house the next morning.

All these thoughts and more wandered through Inge's mind as the bus swayed and bumped its way towards the Swiss border.

"I'm hungry, Inge," Edith said.

Inge glanced at the children seated behind her. All eyes were on her as she pulled her small purse onto her lap. Inge opened it and took out the last of the food that she had kept for this journey. She distributed cheese and bread to the children and then turned back to the window. *May 12, 1944: This would be the most memorable day of all*, Inge thought. She would call this day the day when she reclaimed her freedom.

"What will the Nazis do if they catch us?" asked Henri. He chewed slowly on a soft piece of bread.

"You mustn't think about that," Inge replied.

"But what will they do?" This time, Eddie asked the question.

Inge glanced at little Canari. His face was expressionless. But Inge knew that behind his round, dark eyes, he must be terrified. Or perhaps he was too young to even know the danger facing him.

"I don't know what they will do," Inge replied, looking back at Eddie and choosing her words carefully. "We could be sent somewhere. But maybe, we'll just be sent back to Lyon."

Inge didn't want to think about that possibility either. But she knew that arrest would be the end of the road for her and the other children. If they weren't shot on the spot, they would surely be sent to a concentration camp. After that, who knew what their fate might be?

Inge reached up to wipe her forehead. The bus was warm, but that was not the only thing that made her so sweaty. It was the three layers of clothing she was wearing: underwear, a dress, skirt, blouse, sweater, and jacket. It was easier to carry these belongings on her body than to be hampered with bundles in her arms. Who knew how long they would be hiking from the bus to the border? Instinctively, Inge reached up to touch the shoulders of her jacket. There were treasures hidden inside the lining—precious belongings that only Inge knew about. Inside the lining on her left shoulder was her birth certificate, her real one, with her real name printed on it. Inge would need this document to cross into Switzerland. The lining of her other shoulder held something even more cherished—the silver Star of David that had once belonged to Inge's mother. Just before leaving the Vanvert home, Inge had sewn these two valuable possessions into her clothing. Inge touched both shoulders, feeling the shape of the paper document on one side and the outline of the star on the other. They were her good luck charms, and Inge prayed they would keep her safe as she crossed the border.

The bus was slowing down. *Three hours already*, Inge thought briefly. The time had passed more quickly than she had imagined it would. Once more, she glanced out the window. The bus was skirting the perimeter of the town, heading to the outskirts, and the forest and fields that surrounded it. Even though it was spring, Inge could still see snow glistening on the top of the mountains that rose majestically in the distance. And then, with a final bump and the sharp grating of brakes, the bus came to a stop. There was silence. And then the guide turned to face her.

"Get off," he said, motioning with his head and rising to open the door.

Inge turned to the other children. "Quickly," she said. "Gather your things and follow the *passeur* off the bus." The guide was moving quickly. He would not wait for stragglers. Inge grabbed little Canari by the arm. He was the one she was most worried about lagging behind.

The children scrambled off the bus and began to walk behind the guide. First, they passed through an open field. An old cow grazed lazily in the clearing, raising her head for a moment to survey the hikers before turning back to the grass below her. It was so peaceful in the outdoors; only the sound of birds chirping accompanied the children as they hiked. *How can there be a war going on when this place is so calm and quiet?* Inge wondered. *War could never come to a place like this. Hatred could never live in and amongst these flowers and bushes.*

"Walk quickly and be quiet," the *passeur* ordered from up ahead. His brusque command shattered the silence and crushed Inge's thoughts of peace and solitude. German soldiers patrolled this area. At any minute, the children might run into a platoon of guards, and their escape would come to a quick end. This field was beautiful indeed, but suddenly Inge longed for the cover of thick trees. She clutched Canari's hand even more tightly and quickened her pace.

The children walked silently after the guide in a long, straight line as the minutes passed by, while Inge's eyes darted about looking for soldiers. *The* passeur *must know what he's doing,* thought Inge. *He must know where the soldiers are and when they will patrol in this area.* She had to trust him. She and the others had to follow him without question.

Suddenly, the *passeur* stopped in his tracks and pointed straight ahead. And then Inge saw it—a line of barbed wire stretching in both directions for as far as she could see. They were at the Swiss border!

There was no time to think about what lay on the other side. Henri and Eddie fell to their knees and began to dig in the dirt underneath the wire, scooping up handfuls of loose soil and pushing it off to one side. When they had dug a deep burrow, the boys slid carefully underneath the wire, one after the other. Henri stood jubilantly on the other side and waved. Eddie reached for the wire and carefully pulled it up so that there was more space to crawl underneath.

"Come on," said Henri. "We'll hold it for you."

One by one, the remaining children crawled under the barbed wire and stood on the side of freedom. Inge was the last one to go. She turned briefly to face the guide, not knowing what to say. She felt a strange connection to this distant man who had risked his own life to help the children, payment or not. He merely nodded and then turned to go. In a moment, he had disappeared. Inge fell to her knees and inched her way underneath the wire until she, too, had cleared it.

As she stood up on Swiss soil, her body felt instant relief. Despite the layers of clothing that weighed her down, Inge felt as if she had shed pounds of fear and oppression. Freedom felt light. She turned to grab Edith, hugging her closely. "We made it," Inge whispered. "We're safe."

"Halt!" The loud command startled Inge and the others. She turned to face a soldier who stood in front of her, rifle in his hands. Instinctively, Inge reached out to shield the other children. At first glance, this soldier looked like a German, with his dark-green uniform and his gun extended towards them. And in that instant, all of Inge's feelings of security disappeared. But then, Inge looked more closely and realized that this soldier was Swiss. He would not harm them. Quickly, she explained who they were, and the circumstances of their escape. The soldier nodded.

"Come with me," he said. "I'll take you to the customs building. You all have papers?"

Inge nodded, reaching up once more to touch the shoulders of her jacket. "Come, children," she said. "It's all right. I'm right behind you."

Inge gathered the children and pushed them gently after the soldier. Reluctantly, Canari let go of her hand to walk with the others.

When all the children had moved forward, Inge turned and took one more look at the barbed wire fence behind her. And as she stared at the barrier, she suddenly noticed a soldier standing on the French side that she and the others had just left behind. He was a German soldier on patrol, and a large black German shepherd growled and strained at a leash by his side. Inge's eyes met the eyes of the soldier and they stared at one another for a moment. Then, Inge turned and followed the other children into the customs building.

POSTSCRIPT

Inge, Edith, and the other children were accepted into Switzerland. Inge and Edith went first to a hospital in

Geneva, where they were quarantined for two weeks. Then they were taken to a refugee camp nearby called Au Bout du Monde—The End of the World. They stayed there for one month with refugees from all across Europe.

Eventually, after being moved around several times, Inge ended up in Lugano, where she received word that both her parents had survived the war and were in England. Inge moved to England to be reunited with her parents, whom she had not seen for seven years. There, she met her future husband, Eric Spitz, also a survivor of the Holocaust.

In 1948, Inge and Eric moved to Canada and to Toronto. Her sister, Edith, who had stayed with her after the war, followed Inge to Canada in 1949. Her parents joined her in Toronto in 1951. Inge has three children and six grandchildren. She still has the silver Star of David that she carried with her to freedom.

FULL MOON

• Netherlands, 1944 •
ADA MOSCOVITER WYNSTON'S STORY

Ada at home in Amsterdam, 1939.

"ARE YOU COLD TOO?" Ada snuggled deeper into her sleeping bag, not that it gave her any warmth. The bag was thin, the wool scratchy, and it didn't keep the damp from seeping up from the cement floor. "Rika, are you sleeping?" Ada tried again.

Rika murmured something but didn't open her eyes.

Rika was seven years old, a whole year younger than Ada. They called each other war sisters, because that's what had brought them together—this horrible, mean war that always left Ada feeling like she had stones in her stomach. Rika's parents were kind to her, really, really kind. They had lots of children—Elly, Corry, Adrie, Jan, and, of course, Rika—but no matter how many children were about, and no matter how nice they were, it wasn't the same as having her own brother and sister and her own … *No, don't think about her, don't think.* Ada squished her eyes closed, held her breath, and pushed away thoughts of her mother. Fear was always there, and loneliness too.

"Rika," Ada whispered. This time Ada gave her a good nudge.

Rika moaned a little and wrinkled her nose. Rika always slept soundly, even here in the basement, and she never had nightmares, not like Ada. But then Rika's parents and brother and sisters were safe upstairs in their beds. And Rika wasn't Jewish. Rika didn't understand that the German soldiers who were billeted right above their heads would kill Ada if they found out she was hiding in the cellar. And Rika didn't understand that if Ada did the wrong thing, or said the wrong thing, everyone in the house might be shot. Truth be told, Ada didn't understand either. Not really. She didn't understand why her parents and brother and sister were gone. She didn't understand why she had to hide, or why she would be doing chores or playing dolls or even having dinner and suddenly start to cry.

Two years ago, Ada and her little brother, Sidney, and

sister, Betty, plus Mama, Papa, and a nanny, had lived in a nice house on a nice street in Amsterdam. Mama had a hairdressing shop. Mama was very pretty, tall, and slim, and she was very successful too. Sixteen people worked for her in the hairdressing shop, and even though Mama worked hard all day she was still a good mama. Sometimes, when she came home from the shop, Mama would come outside and play with Ada, Sidney, and Betty, and all the children on the street. Ada had a red pedal car. It was a wonderful thing! Mama would run behind and push her off, and away she would fly down the bumpy road. She could hear Mama call out, "Go, Ada, go!"

Mama liked to laugh. Sometimes, if she really tried, Ada could still hear Mama's laughter. It was deep and throaty and made you want to laugh with her. *Don't think of Mama. Don't remember.* She loved Mama and Papa equally but it was easier to think about Papa.

Papa played the piano in an orchestra. He gave lessons too, and he also played the piano in the movie theatre. Sometimes Ada would go to the theatre with him, and she would turn the pages of his sheet music as the silent movie ran above their heads. When the movie was over, Papa would say, "Ada, you are the best page-turner in the business." *Papa, I miss you, and Betty, and Sidney too.* At night, Mama played the violin and Papa played the piano. They loved each other. It was such a happy life.

Ada jolted upright. She took in a deep breath and held it as she listened to the noises coming from upstairs. *Clomp, clomp, clomp* went the footsteps of the German soldiers in their big boots. It was morning. The German soldiers were up and eating their breakfasts. It was awful having the soldiers in the house, but the army had not asked Rika's parents' opinion before sending the soldiers to live there. Soon they would go off and do what German soldiers did. What *did* they do? Did they go from house to house and take little children from their parents? Did they point guns at people all day, then come back and have supper? Ada hid from the Germans, but sometimes she got a peek at them. They didn't look like monsters. She could hear them talking and laughing. They didn't *sound* like monsters either.

There was more stomping about upstairs, and Ada heard Rika's mother wish the soldiers, "Good day, good day." Over and over. Then the door banged shut. The soldiers were gone. Ada waited. Soon Rika's mother would open the cellar door and tell them that it was time for breakfast. All she had to do was wait.

"Come, girls," Rika's mother called down the stairs. This time, Ada gave Rika a real poke. Rika was sleepy this morning. Usually they were both awake by now.

"Ouch, that hurt," grumbled Rika, but then she smiled. Rika would rather have slept in her nice warm bed, but she knew that Ada would be scared down in the cellar on her own. Two could fight off the monsters in the dark. Imaginary monsters were easy to fight; it was the real monsters that lived upstairs that were the problem.

"Did you sleep well, girls?"

Rika's mother always asked the same question and never really waited to hear the answer. Sometimes Rika would say, "No, Mother, mice nibbled our toes. See? They are all chewed up!" And Rika's mother would absently say, "Good, good." That sent both girls into fits of giggles.

There were lots of breakfast leftovers on the table, even though the German soldiers always stuffed themselves. Rika and her family lived on a farm far away from Amsterdam so there were plenty of eggs, butter, and milk on hand, and they received extra rations because of the soldiers.

A stack of bread sat on the table, and Rika's mother served up leftover sausages and eggs.

"Now girls, chores before play," she said, in her stern mother-voice.

Rika and Ada nodded solemnly, then grinned. They never had to make the beds that the Germans slept in or clean up after them, thank goodness. Except for dishes and sweeping, most of their chores were outside. First they fed the chickens and milked the cows. Next they did errands around the farm for Rika's Papa.

Ada was not allowed to leave the farm, not since last year, when she and Rika had taken bikes to visit a family friend.

Ada had borrowed Elly's bike, which was way too big for a little girl. It took all her concentration to stand on the pedals and make them go around. That's why she didn't see the German soldier standing on the road ahead. He took his gun off his back, pointed it at her, and said, "Are you a Jew?"

Ada swallowed hard, and Rika went pale as snow. But Ada had listened to her war-parents, and she knew just what to say.

"What is a Jew? I live across the street on that farm."

He looked at her blond, frizzy hair and Rika's straight brown hair, tied neatly into plaits. After a very long time—well, it seemed like a very long time—he walked away.

Ada tried to push off on the bike but it was no use. Her legs had turned to jelly. One, two, three turns of the pedals and her bike wobbled into a gooey stream and she was instantly covered in stinky, slimy, sticky, green algae. Ada never left the farm again.

The chores today included churning the butter. That was an awful job, worse than milking the cow, and it took almost forever. Rika's father poured cream into a barrel made of wooden slats held together with metal bands. Then a top was fitted on with a crank handle that had to be turned for hours. Ada and Rika shared the work. As the cream spun into butter, their little arms turned into rubber. Of course there was always the reward. Rika's mother would slather freshly made butter onto two thick slices of bread. The only thing that tasted better was Mama's pear kugel. *Oh, Mama!* It was always this way. Whenever she was thinking about something entirely different, thoughts of Mama would sneak in and her stomach would knot up. But something odd was happening lately. Sometimes she forgot what Mama looked like! Which was worse, to think of Mama and feel sad, or to forget about Mama entirely?

Rika's mother took the lid off the butter churn and pronounced the butter suitable, more than suitable. As promised, each girl received a slice of bread and butter.

"Ummmmm!" Ada and Rika made funny noises until they both nearly fell over laughing.

It was their silliness that made Rika's mother stand back and take a good look at them. "Girls, girls, you are both filthy! Run outside and I'll prepare the bath." Rika's mother clapped her hands, then made shoo-shooing noises. The girls giggled yet again and went skipping out the door.

Their bathtub wasn't like any bathtub in the city. It was outside by the water pump that happened to be in the middle of a long, narrow field. Rika's mother boiled a cauldron of water on the kitchen stove, carried it into the field, poured it into the tub, then added cool spring water to even out the temperature. Both girls stripped down and jumped into the tub. They splashed each other, then rubbed themselves with homemade soap. It was lovely to take a bath outside. Ada closed her eyes and lifted her face to the warm midday sun. Sometimes it was hard to imagine that bad things were happening in the world, that there was a war going on.

She heard a buzzing, like the sound of a fly caught between windows. Ada opened her eyes and stared hard into the distance. Dots, black dots. She squinted and stared harder. Airplanes! They were coming right for them. She looked toward the farmhouse. Rika's mother was waving her arms frantically. Her mouth was moving but her words were drowned out by the hum of the planes. Ada looked up again. There were dozens of planes, more than dozens. They blocked out the sun!

Ada heard the thin whistling of bombs as they dropped in the distance. Then came those other awful sounds—crashing, smashing—and pillows of black smoke rose up all around them.

"Run, girls!" Rika's mother screamed over and over from the kitchen door. There was no time to grab a towel, no time for anything. Both girls leaped out of the tub and ran. The grass underfoot was prickly but they didn't feel it. More bombs dropped. Bombs didn't scare Ada. Nazis scared Ada. And rockets scared her too. Rockets did not make any noise.

Rika's mother ran towards them and grabbed their hands. Her strides were long, and it was hard to keep up. Ada stumbled, but Rika's mama had strong, powerful arms. She grabbed hold of Ada's arm and pulled. Then Ada tripped and fell. Her hand slipped from Rika's mother's grip. *Don't go, don't leave me here!*

The Germans had made Mama close down her hairdressing shop. Jews were not allowed to own or run businesses. Mama hated not working, not doing something productive with her day. Staying home with nothing to do was the hardest thing of all.

"Come, Ada, we'll go visit your cousin," she had said. Maybe Mama hadn't said they were going to visit a cousin, maybe they were going to visit a friend, or maybe they were just going on an errand. It was so hard to remember. It was two years ago, after all. Why did they leave the house that day? Why? Would things have been different if …?

They were on a tram. Ada pressed her nose to the window. The once pretty city of Amsterdam now seemed grey. People scurried from one place to another, heads down, not greeting one another, not saying "Goede morgen," not smiling.

There was a high-pitched squeal as the tram jolted forward then back and came to a sudden stop. German soldiers boarded the tram. Big boots, guns, yelling. The passengers fell silent as the soldiers reached into pockets for their identification papers. Jews did not have to show their papers, the gold star that blazed from their coats said it all.

Two soldiers stood beside the driver and scanned the passengers. These soldiers didn't seem to want to see identification papers.

"Mama?" Ada whispered, but Mama hushed her. There were more German soldiers standing outside the tram, guns trained on the doors.

Ada reached out to her mother. She was only six years old, she needed her mother's hand, her arms, her protection. She wanted to cry out, to bury her head in Mama's coat, to make the monsters go away. Mama pushed Ada's hand away and turned from her, just a little, not so much that her movements could be detected. Why? Why did Mama not hold on to her?

The German soldiers marched down the aisle and pointed to anyone who wore a gold star stitched to their coats, the Star of David. Mama wore a star like that. Ada wore a star too, but her sweater covered it.

"You." A soldier pointed to Mama and motioned with his head. Mama stood up. She didn't look at Ada, she didn't even say goodbye!

Ada thought, Mama, Mama, don't go, but she said nothing out loud. She sat there, paralyzed with fear.

Mama, where did they take you? Where are you now? Why did you push my hand away? I should have gone too. Why didn't you want me to come with you?

Gone, Mama was gone.

"Ada!" Rika's mother turned, grabbed hold of Ada, and pushed her towards the door. The bombs continued to fall. The air was filled with dirt and dust kicked up from the explosions and it was hard to hear, hard to see, hard to think.

There was a muddle at the top of the stairs as all of Rika's brothers and sisters rushed down into the cellar. Ada leaped towards the door. "Oh!" she screamed as she pivoted, then slipped, then fell, bum first, into the butter churn that someone had put right in front of the door. Ada couldn't move. She was stuck. Rika's father swooped down and scooped her up, butter churn and all. The cellar door banged closed behind them.

It took a moment before a match was struck and a lamp lit. All eyes turned to Ada. No one said anything, not at first.

There she sat, naked, in a butter churn.

Someone giggled.

"There, there," Rika's mother said softly to Ada while hushing the other children. She knew well that an eight-year-old girl with a barrel attached to her behind would be mortified.

The barrel made a sort of sucking pop as Rika's mother and father pulled it off Ada's behind. Out popped a buttery bum as yellow as a full moon.

"There, there," whispered Rika's mother again as she covered Ada with a blanket.

Ada would have cried on the spot had it not been for a thought. What would Mama do? Mama loved to laugh, really, she did. And it was awfully funny, when you stopped to think about it. A naked butter-dipped girl, stuck in a barrel in a basement as bombs fell—what could be funnier than that? Ada smiled, then giggled, which was enough to set everyone off in peals of laughter. It was the first time she had thought of her Mama without wanting to cry.

Then Ada had another thought. "Can we save the butter?" she asked. "Do we have to churn more?"

There were planes overhead dropping bombs and shooting rockets, but down below, in the cellar, for one brief moment, there was laughter.

POSTSCRIPT

Ada's mother was taken to Westerbork Camp in the Netherlands and from there to Auschwitz, where she died in the gas chambers after having survived Dr. Josef Mengele's experiments. Ada's father was hidden for three and a half years in one room in Amsterdam. Betty, Sidney, and Ada were hidden in separate places and did not see each other until 1946.

In 1957 Ada immigrated to Canada, where she now lives with her husband, Pierre. Her son, Stephen, lives in the Netherlands with his wife, son, and daughter.

Ada was made a Knight in the Order of Orange-Nassau by Queen Beatrix of the Netherlands. She also received the Governor General's Caring Canadian Award, and the Golden Jubilee Medal on the fiftieth anniversary of the reign of Queen Elizabeth II.

FATHER AND DAUGHTER

· Poland, 1942 ·

ANITA HELFGOTT EKSTEIN'S STORY

Anita in Poland, 1946.

IT WAS THE SILENCE THAT WOKE HER. Was that possible? The window was grimy with soot but still the lights from the ghetto cast a bright glare.

Tata, her father, was sitting on the end of her bed. In one hand he held his round-rimmed glasses, and with the other hand he rubbed his eyes.

"Tata?" Anita was instantly awake.

"They took her, dear girl. They took your mother off the street. She's gone."

"I don't want to leave you, Tata. Please, I don't want to go." Anita reached up to her father. He was so tall and she was so small. Although she was already eight years old, Anita looked no bigger than a child of six.

Tears stood in her Tata's eyes as he shook his head. This was his daughter's only hope.

Tata, once the accountant for the local mill, was now a slave and assigned to rebuilding a bridge that the Soviets had blown up. He had contact with a former officer in the Polish army named Joseph Matusiewicz. He'd taken a chance and asked Joseph Matusiewicz if he would save his little daughter, and Mr. Matusiewicz had said yes.

"Dear child, you must leave. You must." Tata ran his hands through his hair. How did one say goodbye to a little daughter? How had it come to this? It was November 1942, one month after Mama had been scooped up in what the Nazis called an *aktion*, a roundup. Since that day, Tata had been racked with pain, fear, and regret.

"Mr. Matusiewicz is a nice man, Anita. He has a good family who will take care of you. You must do as he says." There was no twinkle in his eyes, no smile on his lips. He wasn't the same Tata who would once upon a time hoist her up on his shoulders and carry her like a princess through their town, who would take her for long hikes, and skiing, and even mountain climbing. Mama didn't approve of the mountain climbing, but nothing could stop them. Anita was an only child, so spoiled, so loved.

They had enjoyed a nice home and a good life, until the Soviets came, and then the Nazis after that. Mama had been forced to give the horrible Nazis her wedding ring, and they'd stripped the fur lining from Tata's coat! Finally, they'd had to give up their home too. There were two hundred families in their small mill town, and every one of them had been herded into a ghetto. Mama, Tata, and Anita had moved into one little room in an apartment.

The Nazis wanted everything and they took everything. They'd already taken her mother away from her, and now they were taking her father too.

Mr. Matusiewicz came for her at night. He was tall, like Tata, and he had blue eyes that turned down in the corners. But he seemed older than her father, more like a grandfather.

"You must leave that behind." Mr. Matusiewicz pointed to the amulet around Anita's neck.

Instantly Anita's hand went to her throat. "No, no, it's from Mama!" She looked first to Mr. Matusiewicz and then to Tata.

"You must not have any identification on you, nothing," repeated Mr. Matusiewicz.

Gently, Tata removed the amulet. "I will keep it for you. Now come, it's time."

It was then that Mr. Matusiewicz pulled out a large potato sack and laid it across the floor. Anita's eyes widened. Was that for her? Was she to be hauled away in a sack like vegetables?

"It will be all right. Mr. Matusiewicz will carry you out of the ghetto in the bag. But listen, Anita, you must not move or say a word, no matter what. Do you promise?"

Tata seemed suddenly stern. Anita bobbed her head and repeated to herself, *Don't cry, don't cry.*

"Come, child." Mr. Matusiewicz, too, was gentle.

Anita stepped into the sack. She was wearing her laced boots, her coat with the soft fur collar, a hat, and gloves.

"Now sit," said Mr. Matusiewicz as he pulled the sack up over her head and tied a knot.

Anita could feel herself being swung up into the air in the sack. Her tummy did a flip-flop. This might have been fun at any other time. In happier days, she would have giggled and laughed out loud. Instead, Anita stuffed a hand into her mouth and bit down hard. The sack swayed back and forth. She mustn't be sick. She was glad not to see Tata's face, glad that she didn't have to wave goodbye.

Mr. Matusiewicz took long strides through the ghetto streets. Anita wasn't cold, not a bit, as she bounced against his back. Was she heavy? And then a thought—what if he just dropped her by the side of the road? He was a stranger, after all, just someone Tata had met in his office. What if this man was playing a trick on them? What if he wasn't going to take her out of the ghetto at all? Maybe he was going to take her to the SS. They would shoot her, and Tata too. *Let me out, let me out!* But she had promised Tata that she would be quiet and still. She had *promised*.

Again Anita felt herself almost flying through the air. She braced for a fall but instead she was lowered carefully onto something soft.

"I'm going to put hay on top of you," Mr. Matusiewicz whispered.

Were they outside the ghetto? She wished he would tell her more. She heard the clopping of hooves, felt a jolt, and heard a horse snort. She was in a cart! They were out and on their way, out … and away from Tata. Anita tucked her knees into her chest and silently cried.

It was the loveliest thing she had ever seen. Well, maybe not quite as lovely as the *Shabbat* candles, but bigger, and, oh, it was just beautiful! The Christmas tree in the Matusiewicz's home was covered in homemade decorations, with red candles clipped to the branches.

When she'd first arrived all she did was cry, but then the days and weeks passed and Christmas arrived. How strange it was, and exciting too. All day Mrs. Matusiewicz cooked and baked, then as soon as she was done she started all over again. There was so little food available, and yet Mrs. Matusiewicz seemed to turn nothing into something.

"Loaves and fishes," said Mrs. Matusiewicz as she kneaded the bread. Anita understood now what she was saying. Mrs. Matusiewicz had told her a story about Jesus, who was the Christian God's only begotten son (what did "begotten" mean?), and how he had taken one loaf of bread and turned it into lots of bread. And he had taken one fish (or was it two?) and made a huge feast. And there had been wine too! There were lots of Bible stories that Anita had to learn now, and there was catechism to memorize, plus a lot of prayers. It was important to kneel when she prayed, and she must remember to fold her hands and close her eyes. She had to be a Catholic girl now.

"Would you like one, Haneczka?" Mr. Matusiewicz held out a plate of Christmas cookies. Anita smiled as she reached for one. There was so much to get used to—her new name, to begin with. She was now Haneczka Jaworska. Anita repeated it to herself every night before she went to sleep—*Haneczka Jaworska, Haneczka Jaworska*—over and over.

Not only was she now Haneczka Jaworska, she was also Mr. and Mrs. Matusiewicz's orphaned niece, whose parents had died in a flu epidemic. That was her new story. So Mr. Matusiewicz became "Uncle" and Mrs. Matusiewicz became "Aunt." And she had a sister too—though not a real sister, of course. Mr. Matusiewicz and Mrs. Matusiewicz— no, no, *Aunt* and *Uncle*—had another niece living with them. Her name was Lusia and she was eighteen, very pretty and a soon-to-be teacher. Lusia was a real niece, and her parents really had died of influenza. There was ten years between the girls, but both had dark, silky hair that curled just a little, huge black eyes, and milky skin. Both were beautiful.

For the moment, with Aunt and Uncle, her sister, home, food, and warmth, Anita—no, *Haneczka*—was safe.

At night, sleeping beside Lusia under a little statue of Jesus on the cross, it was Anita, not Haneczka, who whispered, "Tata, I am here. I am safe. Are you safe? I love you."

"Haneczka, let's hear The Lord's Prayer," said Lusia.

Tonight was a special evening. Uncle was home for a whole day. Uncle was seldom home. Only occasionally did he return for the Christian Sabbath—which, Anita had to remind herself, was on Sunday, not Saturday. Today he brought news of her father. Tata was alive! And to Anita, that was all that mattered.

Tonight, as Haneczka, she wanted to show off her newfound knowledge by repeating The Lord's Prayer perfectly. She clasped her hands together as Lusia had taught her and began slowly. "*Our Father, who art in Heaven, Hallowed be thy name ...*" She got most of the words right but still struggled at the end. Then she crossed herself: *Father, Son, Holy Spirit.*

Lusia clapped her hands, and Aunt and Uncle beamed. Haneczka was proud too. It was important that she learn the prayers, that she become a good Catholic. Everyone was counting on her, Tata included.

Time passed, slowly at first, but things got better. Of course she didn't go out to play. She didn't go outside at all. When someone knocked on the door, Haneczka always ran and hid. But over time, life became easier. Lusia taught her how to read and write. Haneczka helped Aunt with the cleaning, sewing, and cooking, and while she never, not for a minute, forgot about Tata, she didn't cry as much.

And then everything changed again.

It was the winter of 1943, a bitterly cold winter. Haneczka and Lusia were in the front parlour reading books when something out the window caught Lusia's eye. Soldiers! In a blink, Lusia picked up Haneczka and ran to the back window.

"What's wrong?" Haneczka cried. "What's happening?" Haneczka hadn't seen the soldiers, hadn't seen anything, and Lusia did not answer. Instead, Lusia opened the window and threw Haneczka out into a snowbank.

"Run, Haneczka. Run!" hissed Lusia as she slammed the window shut.

Run where? She wasn't wearing a coat or boots. The wind immediately took her breath. Run where? There was yelling inside the house. Run, run! A beaten path led to the outhouse at the end of the garden. She raced towards it, opened the wooden door, closed it behind her, then bolted it shut. Her heart pounded, her breath was short, she was afraid. *Tata, help me!*

With her arms wrapped around her knees she waited in the cold, waited and waited. The sun went down and the moon came out. The bare limbs of trees clattered in the wind, and then, in the distance, she heard gunshots.

The bolt on the outhouse door would not shift. It was frozen in place. No, it was her hands that were frozen. She couldn't get them to work. Again she tried, and again. Finally the bolt slid and the door swung open.

There was light in the house. Haneczka forced herself to walk slowly, then bent down and crawled up the small bank of snow under the back window and peeked in. There was a fire in the stove. Warmth! Aunt was sitting by the fire rocking furiously in her chair. Lusia was pacing up and down. No soldiers. Haneczka lifted her hand and tapped at the window.

Lusia flung her arms around Haneczka. "Where did you run to? The soldiers were watching! We couldn't leave the house to look for you."

Haneczka stood in the kitchen, too cold to even shiver. Her fingers, toes, knees—all numb.

Mrs. Matusiewicz came bustling into the room with a warm blanket in her arms. "Lusia, put more logs into the stove." Together they brought a frozen girl back to life.

"Anita, you can't stay here any longer. It isn't safe," said Mr. Matusiewicz, who arrived home in a frenzy the very next day. "Someone reported that a suspicious little girl lives in this house."

Who would do such a thing? But people did many such things now.

Mr. Matusiewicz had called her Anita, not Haneczka. Hearing her real name was startling, but strangely comforting too.

"They found some Jews hiding in barns. They were shot in the graveyard." Mr. Matusiewicz paused. Anita could guess that he was wondering how much to tell her, whether he should spare her. But she did not need to be told, she had heard the shots, she knew.

"I will try to find another house for you to hide in, but for now I have no choice—I must take you back to your father."

Tata! She could hardly believe her ears. Tata! She would see her father again. Maybe this was what Mrs. Matusiewicz called "a miracle." She would say three Hail Marys, right away.

There was no time to waste. There was no way of telling who had reported them or who was watching the house. Mr. Matusiewicz and Anita left the next morning before first light.

The ghetto was gone. It had been declared *Judenrein*—free of Jews. Only thirty or so men were left to work on the bridge. Tata was one of those men. They were slaves who worked from morning until night with little food and no warm clothes. Tata lived at the back of an old house in a small room with two other men. Each slept on a narrow cot with only a thin blanket for warmth.

Mr. Matusiewicz and Anita stood at the doorway of Tata's cold, mean little room.

"Go on, now," Mr. Matusiewicz said sadly. "Go to your father."

Anita ran. "Tata!"

The look in his eyes was one of astonishment and fleeting joy. He flung open his thin arms and gathered her to him.

The moment of joy was brief, and then agony set in. This was no place for a nine-year-old child. She was in more danger now than ever before.

Every morning, before he went to work, Tata tucked Anita into the bottom of a wardrobe that stood at the back of the room. "You must not get out, Anita. Promise me?" he would say. And she promised. "You must never look out the window, ever. Promise me?" And she promised again.

Wrapped in the thin blanket, Anita waited. It was too dark to read but she had no books anyway. All she could do was sit and wait for Tata to come back.

The days were endless. It was hard not to think of Mrs. Matusiewicz's cooking, or the Christmas goose. Time passed so slowly. The day came when she had to see outside—she just *had* to! One look, that was all, and she wouldn't look long. The sun was out and it was spring. Just one peek.

The cupboard door creaked when it opened. Hugging the walls, she inched over to the window, crouched underneath, then bobbed up. The sun was nice, but there were no flowers or even trees, nothing, really. Disappointed, Anita crept back into the closet and drifted off to sleep.

"Anita!" Tata flung open the cupboard door. "You're here, you're safe." He grasped his chest, and Anita could see that he was trying hard to take deep breaths. Lately he had been complaining more and more about pains in his heart.

Anita leaped out of the cupboard. "Tata, what's wrong?"

Tata stumbled back onto the cot and hung his head. "I thought ... I ... never mind. You were seen, Anita. Not by a soldier, but you were seen looking out the window. Promise me that you will never, *never* do that again."

Tears ran down her face. "I'm sorry … I'm sorry …" But she couldn't finish her sentence because Tata was holding her too tight.

Thunk. That was the sound she woke up to. A dull thud, German voices, a slammed door. Silence.

Anita froze. Not a muscle moved, not a breath was drawn. There was someone on the other side of the wardrobe door. She waited. Minutes passed, then hours. There were no sounds. Was someone asleep out there? What if she opened the door just a little? Just a crack? She could see something. A leg? No, not a leg. An arm, maybe. Who was it? Who was there? Why didn't the man wake up?

"Anita." Tata swung the door open. Before she knew what was happening, she was up in his arms, her face pressed into his shoulder. He didn't want her to see but it was too late. The man who slept in the third cot lay dead on the floor. He had been shot. Anita had spent the day with a corpse.

It was midnight, and Mr. Matusiewicz came to take Anita away for the second time. He had been looking for a place to hide her for months.

It was the spring of 1943 and the war had not yet turned. The Nazis were in full control, and even those few who might have taken in a Jewish child in the past were now paralyzed with fear. But Mr. Matusiewicz had not stopped looking, and he had found her a home with his nephew, a priest who lived near the Soviet border. He would take her there.

"Be a good girl," said Tata. "Be a good girl so that I will be proud of you always." Tata hugged his little girl, hugged her tight.

Anita and Mr. Matusiewicz went off into the night.

Anita never saw her father again.

POSTSCRIPT

Anita lived with the priest and his housekeeper until the end of the war. After liberation, Mr. Matusiewicz was arrested by the Soviets for collaborating with the Nazis and sent to Siberia. He would survive, but would return to his family a changed man. Honouring a promise to Anita's father, however, Joseph Matusiewicz mailed two letters. One went to Anita's aunt in New York City and the other to an uncle in the Belgian Congo. While the effort took years, Anita made her way to Toronto in 1948 to begin a new life.

Anita is still in contact with her Polish rescuers. Today, Anita, widowed after a long and loving marriage, lives in Toronto near her three children and eight grandchildren.

Of the two hundred Jewish families that lived in the mill town south of Lvov, Poland, Anita Helfgott Ekstein is the only survivor.

THE CRATE

Judy and her mother after the war.

WOULD YOU LIKE TO KNOW the one thing I'll always remember about my time in hiding? It's a powerful image, and it has stayed with me ever since that time.

My parents and I were making the long hike up the hillside to a hut that had been built there for us. My father, my Otecko, had arranged it for us, along with a few other families. We were to live in this bunker in the hills, hidden away from Nazis and others who might harm us. Otecko said

118

it would be safe there, but to reach it we had to hike for more than a day. The hills were steep and I knew I had to be strong, but at eight years of age it was hard to be brave and strong when I felt as if my whole life had been turned upside down. We had left our home, my grandparents, and my best friends. They were gone, and now we were escaping into the hills for our lives.

Otecko carried some supplies. So did Mamička,[1] my mother. I carried only the clothes that I wore on my body, and that was enough—two undershirts, three woollen sweaters, two pairs of pants, a skirt, and my winter jacket. It was September 1944, and the weather was mild, but we didn't know how long we would have to be away.

That night, we stopped on a hillside to try to sleep. It was strange to sleep on a slant like that. I wondered if I might roll back down the hill into the village we had left behind. But that wasn't the only thing to worry about. As I lay there next to Otecko and Mamička, trying desperately to sleep, trying not to roll down the hill, trying not to be afraid, it began to rain. That's when Mamička and Otecko gathered their extra clothing and held the pieces over my body. They stayed like that the whole night—standing over me, protecting me from the rain, keeping me dry and safe. That's what I'll always remember about hiding. That's the image I have in my

---

[1] Pronounced Ma-*mich*-ka.

mind—my parents standing over me in the rain, shielding me from harm.

People always ask me if I was afraid during that time, and the answer is *yes!* We were all afraid, and the truth is, there was much to fear. The Nazis could have discovered and arrested us; there were other hostile groups in the hills looking for Jews to torment or kill; we had barely enough food to keep us from starving; and the winter of 1945 was brutal and unrelenting. So, the answer is *yes*, we were always scared. But the difference for me is that I had my parents. I was not alone. And in my heart, I believed that as long as I stayed with them, I would not be harmed. They protected me, watched over me like shepherds guarding a lamb. They kept me secure. They kept me safe.

By February 1945, we had been hiding in the bunker for six months. It felt like six years—like a lifetime. There were other families there, but I was the youngest, and I didn't have much to do with the grown-ups around me. Can you imagine what it's like to have nothing to do all day long, no one to talk to except for your parents, and to live in constant fear that you might be discovered? That's what our lives were like. Mamička tried to entertain me. She told me stories, and I helped her build the fire and clean the dishes in the snow. Otecko and the other men took turns standing guard.

One night, I lay on the bunk bed, trying to sleep. It was terribly cold, and the thin blankets that covered me did little to protect my body from the wind that whipped through the hut. I could hear my parents talking.

"I'm worried about Juditka," Otecko said softly, calling me by my special name. Hearing my father's voice, I began to listen closely, keeping my eyes closed, pretending to sleep so my parents wouldn't notice.

Mamička nodded and glanced over at where I lay. "There's so little for any of us to eat. But Juditka is just a child. She's becoming weaker by the day. I'm afraid she's going to get sick, and then what will we do?"

I didn't move. I lay still, listening to my parents' urgent whispers. My stomach always ached for food, and the little we had was horrible and tasteless. Sometimes I thought that if I had to eat one more bowl of cooked split peas, I would choke. Once, the men killed a horse and cooked it over the open fire. I swallowed the tough meat, trying to be grateful to have something extra in my stomach. Once, my mother had even gone into town to beg for some crusts of bread—that's how desperate we were for food. To pass the time, we would sit around talking about the meals my mother used to prepare at home—*polévka s knedličkamy*, soup with dumplings, or my favourite, *palačinky*, crepes smeared with jam or stuffed with nuts. Talking about food would pass the time, but memories could not fill my empty stomach.

Otecko was talking again, and I listened closely. "Tomorrow, you and Juditka are going to go to the nearest village, to Klačany. She needs food and warmth, or I don't know what will happen to her." Otecko's voice began to rise. He was easily excitable, while my mother always managed to remain calm.

"Won't it be dangerous, Josef?" my mother asked. "Where will we go?"

"I've arranged it all, Šarika," my father replied. "You'll go to Josef Šebo. He's a farmer I know. He will help you, and he'll help our daughter."

My parents continued to whisper while I lay very still, thinking about what they had just said. As much as I hated hiding in the bunker, and as much as I feared being discovered, the thought of venturing into the nearby village was even more terrifying. This hovel had become our sanctuary. Our daily routines here were familiar and predictable. Out there was something else—something I was unsure about. But Otecko had said he had arranged it all, and I trusted my father with my life. Mamička was going with me, so that felt safer. But more important, I really was so very hungry. I could feel the bones sticking out at my hips and shoulders. I felt weak and tired all the time. Maybe this farmer would give me some food. With that thought, I turned in my bunk, pulled the blanket up closer to my neck, and finally fell asleep.

Mamička woke me early the next morning. "Juditka," she whispered. "Wake up. We're going on an adventure today." My mother's voice was calm, as it always was.

I rose quickly. I didn't have to dress because I was already wearing every piece of clothing that I owned. In fact, I had not taken my clothes off once in the six months that we had been here. I rubbed my eyes, pulled my blanket over my shoulders, and followed my mother outside to where Otecko was waiting. He wrapped me in his powerful arms and held me for a moment.

"Stay with your mother," Otecko said. "Everything will be fine, and I will see you soon."

I nodded, remembering that my parents were there to watch out for me, always. Then Mamička and I began the trek through the forest and down the hillside.

On the way, I stumbled and clutched my mother's arm. My legs felt weak and I thought I might fall down. Six months earlier, I had made the climb up this hill with ease. Six months earlier, my legs had been strong; I had been strong. Now, I was so weak with hunger that my legs threatened to give out under me. My head was spinning and I felt dizzy. Despite the cold and frost, the sweat rolled down my back and soaked through the layers of clothing.

"Hold on to me, my darling," my mother said. "I won't let you fall." I held on to my mother and stumbled forward, placing one foot in front of the other, trying to keep my balance, trying to catch my breath.

After what felt like an eternity, we emerged from the forest into the farmer's meadow. I could see the farmer, standing at the far end of the field. As we approached, he glanced nervously over his shoulder and adjusted the cap on his head.

"I've been waiting," he began.

My mother nodded and looked down at me. "It's difficult to walk quickly with my daughter," she said.

The farmer eyed me closely. He was tall and looked strong, probably from years of working in the fields. As I looked up at him, I was startled to see that he had only one arm. The empty left sleeve of his jacket swayed from side to side in the wind. But I had no time to think about this, no time to wonder what kind of accident had maimed him. In the next instant, he reached down with his one arm, scooped me up, and swung me over his shoulder. Carrying me like a sack of potatoes, he turned and marched quickly towards the farmhouse, with Mamička following close behind.

As soon as we walked through the door, a blast of heat from the blazing fireplace greeted my mother and me.

"You poor, poor things," Mrs. Šebo muttered, coming forward to greet us. "I can't imagine how you have been living these past months. You look like you are starving." Mrs. Šebo had a round, kind face. Two small children peeked out from behind her long skirt.

"Thank you for doing this," Mamička said. "We are very grateful for your generosity. Not everyone would help a Jewish family like ours," she added, lowering her eyes.

"Nonsense," Mrs. Šebo replied. "We are only doing what decent people should do. Come. You need to eat, especially your little one here. Then you can wash, and get some sleep."

The soup that Mrs. Šebo placed in front of me smelled heavenly, and tasted even better. I gobbled it quickly, feeling its warmth spread throughout my body. The children watched me with open curiosity. Their clothes were worn but clean, and their faces shone in the glow of the candles on the table. This was a poor family, but I was the one who felt like the pauper. I pulled at my long, stringy hair, knowing that it had not been washed in months. I had lice, we all did, and I tried not to scratch and claw at my scalp and body. This family had so little, and yet they were willing to share everything with my mother and me. We had not experienced this kind of generosity in months, and my eyes filled with tears at their kindness.

When we had finished eating, Mrs. Šebo led us to the small bedroom at the back of the cottage. "My family will sleep in the front tonight. You'll take this room," she said, against my mother's protests. "I've heated some bricks and put them at the foot of the bed to keep you warm." With that, she closed the door to the bedroom.

"Come, Juditka," my mother said finally. "We both need to sleep."

I began to undress, peeling off the layers of my clothing. The clothes fell away from my body in shreds. Then I washed my face and hands in the bowl Mrs. Šebo had left for us. I had not bathed in more than six months, and, try as I might, I could barely scrape a layer of dirt off my body. Finally, I crawled into the big soft bed and nestled close to my mother, grateful as always that she was there with me. The heat from the bricks at the foot of the bed warmed me and I instantly drifted off to sleep.

It felt as if only minutes had passed when I was startled awake by angry voices coming through the small window above the bed. It was early morning; only a sliver of light streamed into the room. I stretched and sat up to look outside, then quickly shrank away from the window.

"Mamička," I whispered urgently. "Wake up! Look outside! The soldiers are here!"

My mother was awake in an instant. She pulled me close to her body and peered carefully out the window. Sure enough, Nazi soldiers had surrounded the village. We couldn't see how many there were, but it looked as if there were soldiers posted at every corner, beside every farmhouse. They held rifles and stood at attention. The townspeople were already up and scurrying through the streets, keeping their heads low and rushing to get back to their homes. Soldiers barked orders and shouted words that we could not hear. I moved closer to my mother, trying to calm the beating of my heart.

Someone knocked at our door and I jumped, wondering if the soldiers had arrived to arrest us. But it was Mr. Šebo, who entered the bedroom and stood awkwardly, his cap in his hand.

"They arrived early this morning," he said, shifting back and forth in the doorway. "They know there are Jewish families hiding in the hills, and they are searching for them. They say that anyone harbouring Jews will be punished and their houses burned down."

My mother rose from the bed and stood to face Mr. Šebo. "We're so sorry for the trouble we are—"

"The important thing is to get the two of you to safety," Mr. Šebo quickly replied. "The Nazis are conducting a search from house to house," he said, moving to the window and glancing outside. "It will be impossible to explain who you are and why you are here. I have to take you to my neighbour's house. He has a barn with a place where you can hide until the danger has passed."

Mrs. Šebo entered the bedroom to join her husband. "Put these on," she ordered, handing my mother some clothing. "You'll need to look like villagers to be able to walk through town. Don't worry, little one," she added, glancing at my face. I had been watching the commotion from underneath the still-warm feather comforter. "We'll keep you safe." She leaned towards my mother and whispered, "Quickly now."

I wasn't fooled. I could feel the tension behind Mrs. Šebo's reassuring words. Even my mother, who always looked calm, was suddenly on edge.

"Mamička?" I began.

"We'll be fine, Juditka. Quickly now, get dressed."

My mother handed me the clothes that Mrs. Šebo had brought in, and I dressed myself in the long pleated skirt and printed blouse. I wrapped the big white scarf around my head and tied it tight under my chin. When I had finished dressing, I turned to look at my mother. We *did* look like simple peasants.

Mamička smiled. "Your own father wouldn't know you right now," she said.

I nodded and followed her into the front room, where Mr. Šebo was waiting. "Stay close to me as we walk," he said. My mother hugged Mrs. Šebo, thanking her over and over for helping us. Then, with a deep breath, Mrs. Šebo opened the front door, and we followed her husband outside.

The streets were alive with people scurrying this way and that. Men rushed to their homes, or out to their fields. Women poked their children to move faster. The tension in the air was thick. Even the cows in the distant pasture seemed on edge, mooing loudly and kicking at the gates that enclosed them. And at every corner, a Nazi soldier stood at attention, barking commands and prodding the villagers to move on.

I kept my eyes down, clutching my mother's hand so tightly I wondered if I might crush her fingers. We kept close to Mr. Šebo, letting him lead us through the streets, past the villagers, and finally to a barn on the outskirts of town. With a quick glance over his shoulder, Mr. Šebo swung the barn door open and motioned my mother and me inside.

"Over here," he said, walking towards a pile of hay in the corner, where bales were heaped on top of one another to form an enormous mound. He brushed some loose hay aside and tugged at several of the bundles until they pulled free. Then, he turned to face us. "Crawl through there," he said. "There's a crate buried inside the hay. Get inside, and close the door. I'll replace the bales of hay, and no one will know that you are here." My mother began to thank Mr. Šebo once more, but he stopped her. "There's no time for that," he said. "I'll come back for you when the danger has passed."

I bent down to peer inside the tunnel that had been left when Mr. Šebo removed the hay. It was dark and not very inviting.

"I'll go first, Juditka," my mother said. "You crawl in behind me." With that, my mother disappeared into the tunnel.

I took a breath and plunged in after her. We emerged on the other side of the short passageway inside a wooden box. It was just big enough for the two of us to sit, crouched over, side by side. My mother pulled me inside next to her and slid a wooden panel across the opening. On the other side of the tunnel, we could hear Mr. Šebo replacing the bales of hay, then footsteps, and then silence.

It was dark inside the crate, but not pitch-black. Some light filtered through the bales of hay and into the box, casting uneven shadows across the floor. Pieces of hay and fine particles of dust drifted down from between the slats of wood. I could not imagine what this crate was for. Had the farmer placed it here just for us? Or was this a hiding compartment for other valuables? My legs began to cramp, and I pulled them up to my chest, shifting on the floor, trying to find a place that was more comfortable. Mamička wrapped her arm around my shoulder and drew me close to her, pulling me into the soft folds of her body.

The last few hours had passed in a blur, without a moment for me to stop and sort out what was happening. I'd just followed the orders of the adults around me. Dress. Walk. Crawl. Sit. A series of commands constructed to save our lives. Hesitate for a moment, stop to argue, and we might be dead—along with the farmer who was trying to protect us. Do as you are told. No time to think. Just act.

But now, for the first time in hours, I took a deep breath and realized the danger surrounding me. On the other side of that short tunnel, just outside those barn doors, Nazi soldiers were systematically patrolling, looking for Jews like my mother and me. I didn't want to imagine what might happen if they found us. That was too much to think about. And so, I buried my head in my mother's shoulder and whispered this thought over and over in my mind: *As long as my mother is here, I'll be safe.* And those words, that prayer, calmed my beating heart.

An hour passed, and suddenly we heard a sound from outside. Someone was removing the bales of hay. I sat up, alert and on edge. Mamička instinctively shifted her body in front of mine, shielding me as we listened to the sound of someone crawling towards us. Another moment passed, and the wood panel in front of the crate was pushed aside. There, facing us, was the farmer who owned the barn. And he did not look pleased.

"You have to leave!" he said abruptly. His face was not angry, just scared, as he glanced back through the tunnel to the open barn. "If they find you here, they'll burn my house down."

"What do you think we're going to do?" my mother demanded. "There is nowhere for us to go."

"It's not my problem," replied the farmer. "I have a family. I need to think of them. Please, just go!"

"No!" my mother said sharply. "We're not leaving."

My mother and the farmer faced off against one another in the dark glow of the hidden tunnel. I looked at Mamička's face; her eyes were calm and her jaw was set. I had seen that determined look on my mother's face many times.

"There is nothing you can do or say to make us leave," my mother continued.

The farmer began to speak and then stopped. I knew he was in a tough position. If the Nazis found us here, he would surely be in trouble. But if my mother and I were arrested out there, he might still be punished if it was discovered, or even presumed, that he had hidden us. He was in danger, whichever way he decided to go. In the end, it was probably better for him to leave us here and hope that we would not be found. Finally, he pulled the wooden panel roughly back in place and then retreated through the tunnel. We heard the bales of hay being replaced and his footsteps disappearing.

I could barely breathe. My mother reached down and squeezed my shoulders once more—a strong, reassuring hug. I moved even closer to her, thinking the closer I got, the safer I'd be.

Barely a minute passed before we heard new voices from the outside. "Search everywhere!" The voices were threatening and harsh. I couldn't tell if the soldiers were inside the barn or circling on the outside, but they sounded close. I shoved my fist into my mouth and held on to my mother with all my might. *What if they hear me?* I wondered. *What if I have to sneeze? What if they poke their guns into the hay, or start to shoot?* Terrifying thoughts streaked through my mind, and I closed my eyes as if I could shut the nightmare out. *How many soldiers are out there? Ten? One hundred?* It didn't matter. What mattered was that we were about to be discovered, and for all my mother's strength and resolve, there would be no way to protect either of us if the soldiers found us.

A minute passed, and the sound of marching boots continued to echo outside our hiding place. And then, miraculously, the sounds began to fade, the voices moved away, and then there was silence once more.

My body went limp. It wasn't the kind of weakness that comes from hunger. It was a relief that came from knowing we were safe. Mamička looked down at me, and in the growing darkness of our hiding place, she smiled the most wonderful calm smile. We remained in the crate for the rest of the day, but I didn't really mind any more. My legs were cramped, and my back was aching, but it didn't matter. What mattered was that my mother was with me, and we were safe.

That evening, Mr. Šebo returned to let us out of the crate. We crawled through the tunnel, left the village, and returned to the hills where my father was waiting.

POSTSCRIPT

Shortly after this incident, Judy and her family decided to leave their bunker and head east, over the mountains to the side of Slovakia that had already been liberated by the Soviets. With much difficulty, they managed to do this, and in the spring of 1945 they reached their home in Humenné. They remained there until 1949 and then went to Paris.

Judy's father came to Canada in September 1949, and Judy and her mother followed a couple of months later. Judy lived in Montreal, Quebec, in Blyth, Ontario, and in Windsor, Ontario, before finally settling in Toronto. Judy is married and has two children and four grandchildren. She studied modern languages at the University of Toronto, and over the years, she has taught French, Russian, and English as a Second Language.

RUNNING

SUSAN LOEFFLER GARFIELD'S STORY

Susan, age 4, in Budapest.

February 1944

Dear Diary,
The Arrow Cross men are so mean. They call themselves
Hungarian soldiers but really they are just Nazis—Hungarian
Nazis. At the beginning of the war Hungary sided with
Germany, but now the Germans occupy Hungary.

Mama and I still live in our old apartment building in Budapest. I want to leave so badly. Papa will find us no matter where we go, I know he will.

Mama and I said goodbye to Papa at the station, not once but twice! He went away to work in some sort of camp for a long time and then he came back home because he was sick. Then he went away again. The last time Papa left, Mama and I were shivering on the platform when the train pulled in. It was so cold my scarf stuck to my lips and my toes hurt when they rubbed against my socks and boots. The smoke from the engine seemed to freeze in the air in great puffs and the train looked like a fire-breathing dragon.

There were lots of people at the station that day—Christians and Jews. It was easy to tell who was Christian and who was Jewish. The Christians were happy. They waved and blew kisses to the people on the train and called out, "Goodbye. See you soon. Have a nice trip."

My Papa was not going to have a nice trip. Papa, like all the Jews waiting for the train, had orders to go back to his military unit. Papa told Mama that likely they would go to the Russian front.

Mama asked him if he had his ticket. It was in the inside pocket of his coat. Even though Papa was going to work for the Hungarian army as a slave-labourer he still had to pay for his own train ticket. Don't you think that was mean?

When the train whistle blew, Papa reached for me and held me so tight I could hardly breathe. Then he stood back and stared at me, like he was trying to memorize me. I wanted to cry. I wanted to scream to all those Christians who pretended they did not see us, "Why are you taking my father away? He is a good man, a good father. Why? Why?"

I could see some of those Christians looking at us, but not directly, sideways. Some of them snickered; they held their hands up to their mouths and giggled. Did they think it was funny that a man was being taken from his family? I was so angry. I wouldn't cry, not in front of him, not in front of all those awful people.

I know that there are some Christian people who don't believe that I am Jewish. I am used to it. Maybe they think that I don't look Jewish. I am small, tiny for my age. I have blond hair, not yellow but the colour of wheat in the field—that's what Papa says. I have very big blue eyes, a tiny nose, an oval face, and a pointy chin—not too pointy. I know I am pretty because everyone pretends that I am not. Mama is afraid that if people tell me I am pretty I will get a big head and become spoiled.

I was eight years old when Papa left and now I am ten, almost eleven. The war has been going on for four years. I can't remember a time when there wasn't a war. That's all the writing I can do for now, Diary. I am tired.

Susan

March 1944

Dear Diary,

We might be forced to leave our apartment soon. They are building a ghetto in Budapest. They want to put us all in a prison. Until it's finished, the government has designated our apartment building a "Yellow Star" house, although some people call apartment buildings like ours Jewish Houses. The soldiers and the police made the superintendent of our apartment building put up a giant Star of David on the gate. I don't like him. He spies on us.

I don't think all Christians are bad. Mama's sister Elizabeth is married to a Christian. He came to our apartment building to take Mama and me away. He argued and argued with the superintendent but we were not allowed to leave. Things would be different now if we had been allowed to go with him.

A letter came from the Red Cross. It said that Papa is "missing." What does that mean? Maybe he ran away? Maybe he is coming back to us?

Mama sits in a chair by the window. The only way she can make any money is by sewing. Her eyes and back hurt and that makes her cross.

Susan

April 1944

Dear Diary,
Every night now, Mama and I lie on our cozy, warm bed with our clothes on. There are airplanes flying overhead. Sometimes they drop bombs. But I'm not afraid of the bombs. I am afraid of the Arrow Cross Militia, the Nazis, and the police. Will they take Mama and me away? What if they take just me? What if they take just Mama? How will I manage on my own?

There is no longer any heat in our building. I am always cold and there is never enough to eat. I keep begging Mama to take me away. "Where would we go, Susan?" Mama asks. I say, "Anywhere, anywhere." Mama just says that we are safer staying put, that without papers we would be picked up and shipped off to a faraway camp. What happens to the people that go to the camps? Everyone I ask says that they don't know, but I know that people who go there do not come back.

Susan

June 1944

Dear Diary,

I am sorry that I do not write more often. It is hard to find a pencil. Pali lives in our building. He is fourteen. He is always trying to see what I am writing in this diary. He thinks I am writing about him. Boys are always thinking about themselves.

Pali says that my father is dead. I told him about the letter Mama received from the Red Cross telling us that Papa was missing. Pali says that missing means dead. He says that no one comes back from the Russian front, especially not Jews. Jews dig ditches and hunt for grenades, but mostly they die.

Pali knows lots of things. He says that in a place called Auschwitz, in Poland, Germans kill people like they kill animals. The grandmothers in the building get angry when Pali says this. They ask, "Why would the Germans kill Jews when Jews can be used as slave labourers?" Everyone says that Pali is spreading false rumours.

We found an old atlas but the name Auschwitz[1] is not on the map, so maybe Pali is making it up.

Susan

---

[1] Oswiecim is the original, Polish name of Auschwitz.

October 1944

Dear Diary,
They came! I was lying beside Mama in our bed when the
Arrow Cross men, the Nazi soldiers, and the local policemen
came. The bell rang but they didn't wait for anyone to answer.
The soldiers started pounding and pounding on the door. And
they yelled too. "Hurry, hurry! Move fast!" Everyone ran out
into the hall. The soldiers pointed their guns at us. Why? We
had no guns, and there were hardly any men living in the
building.

The Arrow Cross mean men took away all the adults
between the ages of sixteen and fifty years old. They didn't want
us children or the old people. They took Mama too. She turned
back and looked at me, like Papa did, as if she wanted to
remember me just as I was. When I tried to run after her she
put her hand up and shook her head. I could read her lips. She
said, "Stay back. Don't follow." Then she was gone. Both my
parents are now gone.

They left us children and a few grandparents in this apart-
ment building—alone. I took you, Dear Diary, and I am hiding
in the basement. Even down here I can hear some of the little
children crying. What will happen to them? What will happen
to me?
Susan

October 1944

Dear Diary,

It's been a week since they took Mama away. Today something horrible happened. There was a high-pitched scream in the hallway. Everyone ran out into the hall. It was hard to see because there is only one dim light bulb but we could hear a woman crying. It was Alana, one of the women who had been taken away with Mama. She and Mama were friends. I ran to her and asked her about Mama. One of the grandmothers grabbed Alana by the arm and dragged her into the apartment so that the superintendent would not see her.

Everyone was begging her for information. They wanted to know where their families were. Alana just kept shaking her head. She didn't know very much. Finally everyone left, one by one, disappointed. She told me that my mother was alive but would not try to escape. Another woman who tried to escape was shot in front of everyone. Alana said that after that, my mother was afraid to run away.

Mama should have tried. She should have.

Susan

November 1944

Dear Diary,

I am in the basement again. I come down here a lot because of the air raids. It stinks down here. There is hardly any water to wash in and most of the toilets are broken. There is an outhouse out back but not everyone can make it, especially the grandparents and the really little children.

There is also a little window in the basement, big enough for me to crawl through if I have to run away. It doesn't matter where. Anywhere would do.

Susan

November 1944

Dear Diary,

I am in the ghetto now. The Arrow Cross mean men barged into the apartment building and made us all come here. I had just enough time to get my little suitcase and you, Diary.

There are lots of people here in the ghetto. It was like walking into a graveyard. I could die in this place. The ghetto is still open. People can walk out. But no one has any place to go!

I haven't seen Pali in days. The boys and girls with no parents were separated from the others. Someone said that there are 70,000 people here, and tens of thousands more in designated "Yellow Star" houses in the city, and maybe more than that in hiding! I don't know if that's true. It's hard to know what's true or false, what is right or wrong, or even sometimes what is good or bad. Outside it is bad to steal, but here it is only bad to steal if one gets caught. Here, children take care of the parents. Children run out from the ghetto and steal food to feed their mothers or grandparents. Everything is upside down.

We sleep on hard benches. There are no beds or blankets and it is very cold. I can feel lice crawling all over me, and there are rats here too. There is talk that the gates will be sealed shut and the entire ghetto will be blown up. I must get out of here. I must!

Susan

December 1944

Dear Diary,
I have a surprise! I am not in the ghetto any more. I just walked out. That's all. The gates were open and they didn't seem to notice me. Was it because I am blond? Was it because I look like a Christian? I took the gold star off my coat. I didn't have any papers. I knew that if I were caught they would shoot me. I was

scared of leaving the ghetto but I was more scared of staying. The only thing I took was you, Dear Diary.

Outside the ghetto the streets were filled with soldiers, Nazis, Arrow Cross, and policemen too. I ran all the way to my aunt's house, the one who is married to a Christian. I got lost a few times but then I found my way. I don't know whether or not she was relieved to see that I was still alive, but I do know that I have put them all in danger.

My aunt said that I couldn't stay with them. She looked so very sad. She said that they were already in danger. My aunt took me to the Red Cross children's orphanage. She said that I will be safe here, but I don't think that I am safe anywhere.

The orphanage is filled with lots of sick children. There are hardly any adults about the place, and there is no food. It's up to the bigger kids to take care of the smaller ones.

Susan

December 1944

Dear Diary,
I've been in the orphanage for a few weeks now. It's horrible, almost as bad as the ghetto. All of us, even the babies, are covered in lice and scabies. Aunt Elizabeth came by a few days ago. She brought a postcard from my mother. Mama is alive! I

know that Aunt Elizabeth is worried about me but she is worried about her own daughter too.

I've explored all over this old building. It's falling down. Just like in our old apartment building I went into the basement and found a window. I think that it is big enough for me to get through—if I have to. I am so scared all the time and I am so very, very hungry.

Susan

December 1944

Dear Diary,

They came. They came! It was night. The Nazis marched into the orphanage wearing their big boots and leather belts, carrying guns. They yelled. All the children, babies too, were to be cleared out. There was another older girl there. She tried to run away. She made it all the way to the corner before she was caught. The soldier who chased her pinned her arms and dragged her back. She pulled and pushed, tears streamed down her face. She was screaming, "Let me go, let me go!" We all watched. I just kept backing up. No one saw me go down the basement stairs. I stood up on a box and bashed in the basement window. Then I climbed out. I was so scared. I ran and ran and ran. I climbed over fences and into backyards. I ran all the way to my aunt's house. I didn't know where else to go! It was dark and I was cold. I threw stones at my aunt's window. My uncle came to the door and took me in. They fed me. I was so hungry.

 Susan

January 1945

Dear Diary,
My uncle took me to the country. I am hiding on a farm now. I think my uncle paid the man to keep me. There is another man here. He is the son of the farmer and he is in hiding too. He ran away from the army. The people are mean to me and I am very dirty. I know I should not scratch but I am covered in lice.

 I heard the farmer say that it will not be long now. The Russians are heading this way. They will be our liberators.

 There are bombs dropping all the time and the sky is filled with planes.

 Susan

January 1945

Dear Diary,

I couldn't stand it any more. I don't care if a bomb drops on my head. The farmers are such horrible people. I left the farm and got on a train to Budapest. The man on the train said that this would be the last train to Budapest. He didn't even ask me for a ticket! He didn't seem to care. When the train pulled into the station in Budapest I ran to my aunt's house. There were bombs and shooting all around. It was so loud. I am so scared.

    Susan

℘

January 1945

Dear Diary,

My aunt washed my head in kerosene to get rid of the lice. It was so awful and I was so embarrassed.

We have no food. I am the only person in the house who can go out and look for food because no one suspects that I am Jewish. I am now saving them. That's funny in a not-so-funny way.

Bombs are falling from planes and there are dead people lying in the streets. I went up to a dead body and looked at it. I made myself look at the body. It was a man.

There are posters on walls with drawings of people hanging from posts. Around their necks are signs that say, "This is what happens to people who hide Jews." There are dead horses lying in the roads too. I saw people come out of their homes with knives. They carved up the horses right on the street. Everyone is hungry. I didn't know what to do, where to go!

And then I saw him—a Russian soldier! He looked like an angel. The Russians are our liberators. The Nazis are beaten!

I am alive and we are free, Dear Diary. I don't remember what peace is like. All I remember is war.

Susan

The international ghetto and the central ghetto in Budapest were liberated by the Soviets in mid-January 1945. About 94,000 Jews remained in the two ghettos, another 20,000 came out of hiding, and another 20,000 returned from labour camps. Nearly fifty percent of Budapest's Jewish population died during the Holocaust.

POSTSCRIPT

Susan's mother survived life in the camps, only to die of typhus while walking back to Budapest. Susan lived with her aunt after the war and went back to school. In 1948 the

Canadian Jewish Congress brought a group of orphans to Canada. Susan was amongst them. After the death of Susan's grandmother and during the Hungarian Revolution in 1956, her aunt immigrated to Canada.

Susan has two daughters, a son, and six grandchildren, three boys and three girls. After forty years of marriage, Susan lost her husband. Today, Susan is still tiny, still blond, and lives in Winnipeg, Manitoba. She is happily remarried.

LETTERS TO
MAM AND PAP

• Holland, 1943 •
CLAIRE FRIEDBERG BAUM'S STORY

Left: *Claire and her sister, Olga, with liberating Canadian soldiers.*
Right: *Claire and her sister, Olga, with Tante Nel.*

How long have I been hiding? How many days, months,
and even years since I said goodbye to Mam and Pap? I
remember 1940 when the bombs fell in my city of
Rotterdam. Houses crumbled and thousands of people were
hurt or killed. I heard the sound of the bombs dropping
even though I covered my ears and closed my eyes tightly. It
was terrifying.

After that, things got very bad for Jewish families like mine. We couldn't go to public school. We couldn't shop in stores or be outside after dark. When the Nazis started arresting Jewish families, that's when Pap decided we needed to go into hiding. Pap told me just like that. He said, "You and Ollie are going away. You'll be safe together." I didn't ask any questions. Something told me not to—a look in Pap's eyes, and the way he exchanged glances with Mam.

"Don't tell *anyone* you are Jewish," Mam warned before we left.

"And don't talk to strangers," added Pap.

I didn't want to say goodbye to them. I didn't want to leave without them. Ollie kept saying we were going on a holiday. She sang this over and over as if it were a jingle. But my little sister is only four years old and she doesn't understand these things. I am six.

November 1942

Dear Pap,
I want to wish you a happy birthday. I hope you have a very nice day, and Mam too. I am sending you a card. It is very nice and I coloured it in myself. I hope you will be happy with it.
Goodbye Pap and Mam,
Many kisses,
Clary

Ollie and I are living with Tante Nel. My sister's real name is Olga, but we call her Ollie. Tante Nel says that Ollie and I must write letters to our parents, to tell them what we are doing and to let them know that we are okay. We don't know where our parents are. We don't put an address on the letters. All we know is that Mam and Pap are also hiding somewhere with someone. I hope their family is as nice to them as Tante Nel is to us. She has kind eyes and a beautiful smile and she hugs me when I am sad, just like Mam used to do.

"If anyone asks where your parents are," warns Tante Nel, "you must say that your father is working in Germany and your mother was hurt in the bombing of Rotterdam, and that she is in the hospital. That's why you have come to live with me, your Tante."

Tante Nel is not really our aunt, but we are pretending that she is, just as we are pretending to be Protestant. Tante Nel has a husband, but he is working in Germany. She doesn't have any children. That's why I think she likes Ollie and me so much. We are the children she wishes she had.

Tante Nel's parents live next door, along with her brothers. It is one of her brothers who takes our letters to Mam and Pap. He must know where they are hiding, but I'm not allowed to ask. We call Tante Nel's parents Oma and Opa, which is what we used to call our own grandparents before they disappeared, taken away by the Nazi soldiers.

Tante Nel's mother reads the Bible to Ollie and me three times a day, after breakfast, lunch, and dinner. She prays all the time, and she tells me to pray also for food and other things. She tells us to pray for miracles. She believes in miracles. Even when the chickens lay eggs, she thinks that is a miracle—and sometimes so do I! Oma has black stockings and a black dress. She has a hearing aid that looks like a big horn that is attached to a long tube. She puts the tube in her ear and rests the horn on the table. I must talk loudly and clearly into the horn so the sound can travel up the tube, and she can hear what I say. You would think that all of that would be scary. But Oma is very kind, and listening to her read the Bible is like listening to stories read aloud. And when I listen to the Bible stories, it stops me from thinking so much about Mam and Pap.

May 1943

Dear Mam and Pap,
I made a scene in a shoebox today. I made a little table and chairs from paper, and drew pictures on the wall of the box. I pasted paper snowflakes on the outside. When you look inside a small hole on one end of the box, it looks just like a real kitchen inside. Now it is school time and we can't go outside. But when it is twelve o'clock I will go outside with my box.
  Many kisses,
  Clary

I am not allowed to go to school. It is too dangerous. Someone might guess that I am Jewish and then I would be arrested, and so would Tante Nel. Tante Nel is teaching Ollie and me to read and write. She is also teaching us how to knit. Sometimes, she draws a picture on a piece of cardboard. Then she pokes holes around the drawing and I sew around the picture with thick coloured yarn. I will send one of the pictures to Mam and Pap. Jopie also comes to teach us to read and write. Jopie is a friend of Tante Nel's. She is pretty and has a nice smile and she says that my handwriting is beautiful and very grown-up.

Some days, it is so boring to be inside all the time. There is nothing to do and no one to play with except for Ollie. And we don't have any toys at all, only our own imaginations. So, we play pretend all day long. I'm good at it, just like pretending not to be Jewish, and pretending that Tante Nel is my real aunt. Ollie and I can turn a bedsheet into a tent, or a curtain, or a special hiding place. When we play pretend, I am always the mother, and Ollie is the father. That way I can be the one who looks after everyone and takes care of things, just like I think I need to take care of Ollie.

When school is finished for all the other neighbourhood children, then we are allowed to go outside and play. But even with the other children, we must continue to pretend. They must think that we have been at school during the day, just like them. I listen carefully to what the girls ask me and

I know how to answer. If someone says, "We got pencils in school today," I say, "Oh, we got pencils in school too. Were yours red?" I am good at make-believe. But sometimes I wonder: Do these girls really believe that we are just like them? Do they realize that I am pretending all the time? Can they guess that we are Jewish?

December 1944

Dear Mam and Pap,
On Ollie's birthday, some girls came over. We gave them candies and played with them. We also had cake and did it ever taste good. I have received a few toys—a little chair, a chess-board, and a doll with a beret. I also got a little book. For Christmas, we have a Christmas tree. It has birds on it and balloons and a little toadstool. For the time being, I'm still okay. We wish you all a Happy New Year. Bye Mam and Pap.

Many kisses,
Clary

Tante Nel has chickens and rabbits in the yard. She even gave us our very own rabbits to take care of. Mine was black and white and Ollie's was brown. My black-and-white rabbit was beautiful and soft, and very cuddly. I fed him radishes and carrots and I brushed his soft fur until it shone. I never had a pet before and I loved him. But on Christmas, a terrible thing happened. Tante Nel said that we were going to have to kill the rabbit and eat it for Christmas dinner.

"No," I cried. "You can't kill my beautiful pet!"

But Tante Nel said there wasn't much food to eat because of the war and because she didn't have any ration cards for Ollie and me.

"I'd rather starve," I shouted at Tante Nel, even as my stomach growled and I longed for food.

Tante Nel decided that we would draw lots. She put two sticks in her hand and told Ollie and me to each pull one out. The one who chose the longer stick would get to keep her rabbit. I pulled out the shorter stick.

That night, before we went to church with Tante Nel, I hugged my rabbit harder than I had ever hugged him before. I whispered in his ear that I was sorry and that I would never forget him. Church was beautiful that night. There was a Christmas tree in the front and we were allowed to stop and look at it. But all I could think about was my pet rabbit.

When we got home, there he was, roasted and sitting on the table. I couldn't even look. I felt sick and asked Tante Nel if I could go to bed. She said that I must eat. She said I must be grateful that my rabbit had provided us with nourishing food. But I couldn't eat the rabbit. I would rather have gone to bed with my aching stomach than take a bite of the food.

January 1945

Dear Mam and Pap,
I have a nice present. The rabbit had eleven young ones. They
are all big and two have already died. Jopie has been here. The
chickens have laid eggs and they ate one of the eggs themselves.
Don't you think that was naughty? Now I will stop writing.
  Many kisses,
  Clary

Ollie and I get our clothes from the trading bureau.
When my shoes or dresses become too small, Tante Nel can
take them to the trading bureau and get another size. So, we
usually always have clothes that fit us, even if they aren't
new. But we never have enough food and I am hungry all
the time. Tante Nel has ration stamps that she uses to get
food. It costs so many stamps for meat, bread, and then
basics like flour and sugar. Tante Nel is always running out
of ration stamps, so she goes to a farm that is far away and
she trades with the farmer. She gives him clothes and he
gives her food. She travels on her bicycle for many miles to
the farm. I don't want to complain to Tante Nel, but I am
always hungry. Once I went to the soup kitchen, but all I got
was a bowl of grey mush. I could barely eat it. My stomach
feels empty all the time, and it hurts. But I would still never
eat my rabbit.

February 1945

Dear Mam and Pap,
How are you? How are you making out? We have been to the
circus and it was so cute. There was a lady on a swing turning
so quickly with lights on her skirt. I am pasting a few pictures
here for you that I cut out of a book. One is a picture of two
little girls. You can pretend that it is Ollie and me. And here is
a picture of a little dog that I wish we could have.
　　Many kisses,
　　Clary

Once, we were able to go to the circus with Tante Nel. But
there was a sign on a big yellow banner with black letters that
said, "This Place Is Forbidden to Jews." It frightened me, and
I didn't want to stay. It is very dangerous to be staying here
with Tante Nel. Sometimes I forget that there is a war going
on, and that Jewish people are being arrested all the time.

When we are in Tante Nel's house, we are not allowed to
look out the windows. "If the soldiers see you, they will shoot
you," she warns. We can't even look out the windows that are
at the side of the house, even though they are not close to the
street. There are mirrors on the outside wall close to these
windows. Someone walking by might see our reflection in
the mirror and know we are here. The Nazi soldiers are
patrolling on the street all the time. They can walk up to

anyone and ask for identification papers. If you don't have them, you can be arrested. Ollie and I don't have identification papers. That's why no one can see us.

There are blackouts every night. The lights in the city go out so that planes won't know where to drop their bombs. But I can hear the sound of rockets and bombs falling nearby. It scares me. It reminds me of the time the bombs fell in Rotterdam and everything was destroyed. I cover my ears and try not to hear the sound of the bombs, but I still can.

Every night we put our shoes by the side of our beds, just in case there is a raid and we have to run somewhere quickly. Tante Nel is always afraid of raids. One day, we heard that there was a raid in the neighbourhood. Nazi soldiers were going from house to house, looking for people to arrest. That day, we knew the soldiers were getting closer and closer to Tante Nel's house. She came running into our bedroom looking more scared than I had ever seen her.

"Hide somewhere!" she shouted.

Ollie and I grabbed our shoes and ran with Tante Nel next door to Oma and Opa's house and we stayed there, waiting to see what would happen.

The soldiers—four of them—sat down on the front steps of the house to eat their lunch. I could see them sitting there, even though I wasn't supposed to look. They were laughing and joking with one another. Ollie was shaking next to me, and I was scared too. I thought that any minute they would bang on the door and walk inside. They would point a gun at my head and I wouldn't be able to pretend any longer.

When the soldiers finished their lunch, one of them pointed to Oma and Opa's house and said, "I suppose we should search in there now."

But the other one shook his head. "No," he said. "I think we've already searched that house."

"Are you sure?" the first soldier asked.

"Positive," the other replied.

And then, the soldiers gathered their guns and walked away. Can you believe our luck? They missed the house where we were hiding because they thought they had already searched inside. I was still shaking, even when Tante Nel grabbed me and hugged me close. Someone must have been watching out for us. Perhaps it was a miracle, just as Oma says.

April 1945

Dear Pap and Mam,
Tante Nel got us slippers today from the trading bureau. Thank you for the nice shoes and socks. I have a new bow in my hair—
Ollie too. I made you a bookmark and I am sending it to you.
The socks were so nice and the paper doll that you sent too. I've
already cut it out. Tante Nel bought chickens. They are already
eight days old. When they are six months old, Tante Nel says

they will lay eggs. We sometimes do get a little egg from Tante Nel. We've had tomatoes. Tante Nel baked bread with a lot of sugar. It was very good. She also made pancakes. Tante Nel says she will buy us three new rabbits.

Many kisses,

Clary

It is May 5, 1945. I know this date because we have been living with Tante Nel for three years now. But an amazing thing has happened. This morning, when Ollie and I woke up, there were loud noises on the street. At first we thought it was the Nazi soldiers and there would be another raid. I started to reach for my shoes so that I could run and hide. But then I stopped. This was a different kind of noise. The shouts sounded happy.

Tante Nel says we can look outside, and at first, I don't believe her. We have never been allowed near the window. But Tante Nel is smiling, and when I look outside you can't imagine what I see. There are soldiers and jeeps rolling down the centre of the street. But these are not Nazi soldiers with their ugly flags. These are Canadian soldiers, and they are waving their colourful Canadian flags. Everyone is jumping up and down and hugging each other. And the people are shouting, "The war is over! We are free!"

I want to be outside too. I want to jump up and down and scream and shout. But Tante Nel has just come back from the farm with food. We have not had a meal in a long time, and Tante Nel insists that we eat before we go outside. How can I eat when all of this is happening? Tante Nel feeds us mashed potatoes and applesauce. The food tastes wonderful, but it sticks in my throat and I can't finish it fast enough.

Suddenly, there is a knock at the door. At first, I am frightened. Even though I hear the shouts of freedom, I am afraid that Nazi soldiers might be coming to arrest me. But Tante Nel tells me to answer the door. And when I do, there are two strangers standing there, a man and a woman. They are pale and thin and they huddle together.

"You look so funny!" I blurt out. But then, something stops me. There is something so familiar about this man. And I have seen this woman's smile before. I cry out and fly towards my Mam and Pap, with Ollie close behind me.

Now I know for sure. The war is over. I am safe and in the arms of my parents.

POSTSCRIPT

Claire and Olga lived safely with Tante Nel for three years while their parents were hidden in another location. After the war, Claire and Olga returned with their parents to live in Rotterdam. They waited for other members of their family to return, but most of their extended family, including their grandparents, did not survive the war.

In 1951, Claire and her family left Holland to move to Canada, the land of their liberators. Claire lives in Toronto with her husband. She has three children and eight grandchildren. She always stayed in touch with Tante Nel. Sadly, Tante Nel passed away only weeks after this story was written. Some years ago, Tante Nel was honoured in Israel as "Righteous Among the Nations" in recognition of her having risked her own life to help save the lives of Claire and her sister.

About twenty years ago, Claire received a package in the mail from a woman in Holland. She had found some letters and drawings in the cellar of her home. This was one of the homes where Claire's parents had been hiding. These were all of the drawings and letters that Claire and Olga had written to their parents during the three years that they lived with Tante Nel.

One of the pictures that Claire sent to her parents.

Now that you have heard our stories, you are a witness too.

—JUDY COHEN, HOLOCAUST SURVIVOR

GLOSSARY

Adolf Hitler Born in 1889, Hitler came to power in 1933 when he was elected Chancellor of Germany. Hitler promised to restore prosperity to the German people following their economic devastation in the First World War. Under his leadership, Germany invaded Poland in September 1939 to begin the Second World War. His racial policies culminated in the killing of more than 6 million Jews and more than 5 million other people. He committed suicide in the final days of the war in 1945.

AJS The Armée Juifs Secret, or Underground Jewish Army, was a secret Jewish Resistance organization in France that worked to help other Jews. The AJS sought out Jews who were in hiding and provided them with food stamps, falsified papers, food, and clothing.

Aktion A term that refers to the rounding up and deportation of Jews to concentration camps.

Allies The countries that joined forces in an alliance to oppose what were known as the Axis powers (see Axis powers). The Allies included the United States, Great

Britain, the Soviet Union—known as "the big three"—Canada, France, South Africa, and many others.

Arrow Cross A pro-Nazi party led by Ferenc Szálasi that ruled Hungary in 1944 and 1945. In this short time, 15,000 Hungarian Jews were murdered, and 80,000 deported to the death camps. After the war, Szálasi and other Arrow Cross leaders were tried and convicted of war crimes.

Axis powers The three major countries opposed to the Allies were Germany, Italy, and Japan. The term "axis" came from Benito Mussolini, the Prime Minister of Italy during the Second World War. He said that Germany and Italy would form an "axis," and other countries in Europe would revolve around this partnership.

Benito Mussolini The Prime Minister of Italy from 1922 to 1943, Mussolini became a close friend and ally of Adolf Hitler and brought Italy into the Second World War in 1940 on the side of Nazi Germany. Italy was defeated in 1943. In 1945, Mussolini tried to escape Italy for Switzerland. He was captured and killed.

Bergen-Belsen One of the Nazi concentration camps located in Germany. Over the course of the war the camp held Jewish prisoners, prisoners of war (POWs), political prisoners, Roma (Gypsies), Jehovah's Witnesses, and homosexuals. More than 100,000 prisoners perished there, including Anne Frank and her sister, Margot. British forces liberated the camp on April 15, 1945.

Bunker A building or shelter meant to protect and hide individuals. Jews built bunkers in the forests, where they hid to avoid being killed or deported to the concentration camps. Some bunkers were built underground; some were above-ground structures. Many were stockpiled with supplies to last for months.

Château de la Guette Château de la Guette was a mansion near Paris owned by Edouard and Germaine de Rothschild. Between March 1939 and May 1940, after Kristallnacht, La Guette served as a home for 130 German Jewish refugee children between the ages of nine and fifteen.

Collaborator Anyone who co-operates with an outside or enemy force against his or her own country or political group.

Concentration camps The prison camps, death camps, and labour camps where Jews and other people were sent. Hitler established more than one hundred major concentration camps and several thousand smaller camps.

Fatherland One's native country or homeland. During the Second World War, the term was most commonly used as a patriotic reference to Germany.

Gestapo The short term for *Geheime Staatspolizei*, or the Secret State Police of Germany. The force was established in 1933. Under Hitler, the Gestapo had the power to operate in whatever way they wished. They could arrest, confine, and interrogate anyone who was thought to oppose Germany's political position. They also were responsible for setting up and administering the concentration camps.

Ghetto The enclosed area of a city or town that separated Jews from the rest of the community. Between 1939 and 1945, Hitler established 356 ghettos in Poland, the Soviet Union, the Baltic states, Czechoslovakia, Romania, and Hungary.

Josef Mengele The concentration camp doctor in Auschwitz, he was known as "the Angel of Death." Mengele was in charge of the selections. He also masterminded a series of scientific experiments using Jewish prisoners as subjects. Most of his victims died in these human experiments. He escaped to Argentina at the end of the war, and died in an accidental drowning in Brazil in 1979.

Kristallnacht On the night of November 9, 1938, a violent, organized assault was conducted against Jews in Germany and in parts of Austria. Gangs of Hitler Youth and soldiers roamed the streets, raiding Jewish homes and shops and beating up Jewish citizens. Buildings and synagogues were set on fire and destroyed, leaving the streets covered in the shattered glass from smashed windows. The name Kristallnacht means "The Night of Broken Glass."

Lice Lice are tiny insects that burrow into the scalp and other places on the body. Lice spread quickly and easily from person to person in conditions where hygiene is poor. Left untreated, this could lead to typhus and possible death.

Marshal Tito Born Josip Broz Tito in Croatia, he was a Yugoslav revolutionary who organized and led the resistance movement known as the National Liberation Movement during the Second World War. He served as leader of the Socialist Federal Republic of Yugoslavia from 1945 until his death in 1980.

Nazi The short form for *Nationalsozialistische Deutsche Arbeiterpartei*, or the National Socialist German Workers' Party. This was the political party of Adolf Hitler.

Partisans Partisans were members of underground resistance organizations that worked to sabotage the Nazis. They were also known as "freedom fighters" or "Resistance fighters."

Refugee A person who is forced to leave his or her home because of war or persecution and seek protection in a safer place.

Resistance See Partisans.

Righteous Among the Nations This honorific recognizes those non-Jews who risked their lives to save Jews during the Holocaust. The title was first established in 1963. Those selected for this honour are awarded a medal and a certificate of honour, and their names are added to the Wall of Honour in Jerusalem at the Holocaust Memorial Museum.

SS An acronym for the German word *Schutzstaffel* or "protection squad." This force was created in 1925 to be Hitler's bodyguards and later became the elite unit of the Nazi Party. Members of the SS staffed the concentration camps, the police, and the military.

Star of David The six-pointed star that is the symbol of the Jewish religion.

Swastika The symbol of the Nazi Party, which appeared on the flag of Nazi Germany during the Second World War. The swastika symbol is also found throughout the world in various religions and cultures, where it has different meanings.

Theresienstadt The German name for the town of Terezin. Located approximately ninety kilometres northwest of Prague in what is now the Czech Republic, this town became a ghetto in 1941. More than 150,000 Jews were imprisoned here, including 15,000 children. Close to 100,000 were deported to the concentration camps. The Soviet Red Army liberated Theresienstadt on May 8, 1945.

Westerbork Camp Located on the border between Germany and the Netherlands, this is a camp where, during the Second World War, Dutch Jews were assembled before being sent on to concentration camps. Anne Frank lived there before being sent to Auschwitz.

ACKNOWLEDGMENTS

We are indebted to the survivors and their families who allowed us to interview them and write the stories included in this collection: Adam Fuerstenberg, Esther Schwabenitz Bem, Alexander (Joshua) Levin, Fée Beyth Goldfarb, Sally (Sarah) Barath Eisner, Inge Rosenthal Spitz, Ada Moscoviter Wynston, Anita Helfgott Ekstein, Judy Jakubovic Schachter, Susan Loeffler Garfield, and Claire Friedberg Baum. You inspire us with your candour and your courage.

Many thanks to the talented and dedicated staff at Penguin Group (Canada) who have been part of this project from the beginning: Jennifer Notman, Catherine Marjoribanks, Eleanor Gasparik, David Ross, and Lisa Lapointe. Finally, to Judy Cohen, who went the extra mile.

As always, we are grateful to our families and friends, whose love and encouragement sustain us beyond measure.